THE CHARISMATIC SPIRITUALITY
OF ABRAHAM JOSHUA HESCHEL

Mystical Teachings of an American Rabbi

THE CHARISMATIC SPIRITUALITY
OF ABRAHAM JOSHUA HESCHEL
Mystical Teachings of an American Rabbi

S. Daniel Breslauer

The Edwin Mellen Press
Lewiston•Queenston•Lampeter

Library of Congress Cataloging-in-Publication Data

Breslauer, S. Daniel.
  The charismatic spirituality of Abraham Joshua Heschel : mystical teachings of an American rabbi / S. Daniel Breslauer.
    p. cm.
  Includes bibliographical references and index.
  ISBN-13: 978-0-7734-2531-6 (hardcover)
  ISBN-10: 0-7734-2531-4 (hardcover)
  1. Heschel, Abraham Joshua, 1907-1972--Teachings. 2. Spiritual life--Judaism. I. Title.
  BM755.H37B74 2011
  296.3092--dc23

                              2011041367

hors série.

A CIP catalog record for this book is available from the British Library.

Front cover: Rabbi Abraham Joshua Heschel
(Courtesy of the Library of the Jewish Theological Seminary of America) Google.com

The Edwin Mellen Press   The Edwin Mellen Press
        Box 450   Box 67
   Lewiston, New York   Queenston, Ontario
   USA 14092-0450   CANADA L0S 1L0

                   The Edwin Mellen Press, Ltd.
                   Lampeter, Ceredigion, Wales
                   UNITED KINGDOM SA48 8LT

             Printed in the United States of America

In Memory of Esther Gurian

April 9, 1910 – September 5, 2008

TABLE OF CONTENTS

Poets often consider the effect of art on those perceiving it. John Keats, reflecting on a Grecian urn concluded that "Beauty is truth, truth beauty." An archaic torso of Apollo led Rainer Maria Rilke to the lesson that "You must change your life." My effort in the various articles and books I have produced has been different. While I write about "ethics" my concern is less prescriptive than descriptive. I hope to provide readers with insight into themselves and their lives. These readers, I believe, act more morally, more consistently, and more honestly than they themselves recognize. I hope by providing images with which to identify they will find a new means to affirm themselves and their ideals. This conviction and hope helps explain why I tend to fill my books with tales and stories and with people and situations.

This present book follows a similar pattern. As with my previous works this one draws on the Jewish tradition, because I know those sources best. Unlike my earlier writings, however, I hope to address a general audience and offer images available to all people. The virtues I sketch—the flexible self, compassion, generosity, and skepticism—are accessible to anyone. If the stories I relate have Jewish heroes and make reference to Jewish ceremonies or events, these can translate into touchstones from other traditions.

The decision to address this general audience grows out of my attachment to the iconoclastic efforts of Abraham Joshua Heschel on whose American presence as a religious maverick I wrote my Ph.D. dissertation in 1974. During my early engagement with Heschel's writing, I was asked why I preferred his ideas to those of Martin Buber. At the time I did not know how to respond. I know now that what I found in Heschel was a way to root my Jewish commitments in a universal concern. Heschel's influence has pervaded all my writings, whether explicitly or implicitly. I do not claim to be either an "expert" on Heschel nor a disciple; he stands neither as a "Jewish father" to me nor a mere intellectual mentor. Instead he remains a catalyst, a gadfly, provoking me to new thinking. This book reflects that influence. While both the title and every chapter in this book refers to Heschel, the content is less an exposition of his thought or a critical review of his ideas than a working out of implications and hints that have occurred to me while reading his writing. Heschel was, of course, an "ethical scholar," a teacher who understood the classical, medieval, and modern ethical traditions, both Jewish and non-Jewish, and was a careful student of this material and an astute interpreter. His legacy in expanding insight into Jewish ethics remains impressive and undiminished. Nevertheless, his greatest influence came when he fearlessly crossed religious boundaries to face what he saw as a general spiritual crisis—a crisis facing all religions. Heschel clearly advocated action on the part of both religious leaders and adherents. He did take specific social and political stances. His ultimate aim, however, was to change and spiritualize the individuals to whom he spoke. I agree with Heschel that the crisis is general and goes beyond traditional boundaries and therefore use his category of "depth-theology" as a basis for my analysis.

Heschel never gave a precise definition for the concepts making up depth-theology. He pointed to its origin at the

ii

foundation of all religions and at the most basic responses of human spirituality. I go beyond this intuition to flesh out at least four elements of such a basic spirituality common to all human religiousness. I am not arguing that these are the only elements involved, but I do want to argue that they are essential ones. I illustrate those elements using tales derived from the Jewish tradition and examples drawn from Jewish thinkers, both modern and pre-modern. Many of the sources come from the tradition of the Kabbalah, a tradition that has been called "mystical." By mystic I have in mind the prophetic tradition of challenging the status quo and demanding more than ordinary spiritual commitment. I use the terms "mysticism," "spirituality," and "prophetic charisma" as equally useful ways of referring to that attitude of iconoclasm. In that usage I feel that I am being consistent with Heschel's teachings and the insights he discovers in the Jewish tradition.

Heschel, the stories presented, and the thinkers cited all use theological language. They construe spirituality as a human responsive to the divine. The well-known tale of the blind men and the elephant expresses the confusion associated with notions of divinity. The word "God" refers to various realities depending on the nature of a person's spirituality. I applaud each of the distinct ways in which people appropriate this term. This variety of usage need not undermine belief in a single deity. People's beliefs mirror their encounter with the world and their construction of reality.

The idea of a divinity or a God often takes an anthropomorphic form—expressing abstract concepts in human terms. In earlier ages such an approach permitted an audience to gain access to these concepts using images they found familiar. While many people today still find these images compelling, others do not. For these others, this book offers alternative approaches to the reality indicated by the term "God." Heschel, explicitly, and other sources indirectly, provide a more modern bridge to familiarity—anthropopathism rather than anthropomorphism. Anthropopathism understands the deity in terms of human emotions rather than in terms of physical images.

Not all readers require this way of looking at divinity. Nevertheless, many may find it a help to reflect that the term "God" refers collectively to the emotional environment within which all human beings live and which not only shapes them but is shaped by them. Responses such as compassion, generosity, and skepticism seem rooted in reality, not just in this or that arbitrary individual motivation. By God Heschel, as well as others, refers to the sense that these emotions mirror tendencies within the world, not just the individual. This "functional" definition does not necessarily reject other ways of understanding divinity. It coexists with them and allows alternative meanings to the word God.

Throughout the book I refer to charismatic spirituality as the result of these emotions, as what Heschel would construe as answers to a divine pathos. This spirituality is both religious and theological because it moves beyond the particular human being experiencing the emotion to valorize that emotion itself as valuable and worthwhile. To call charismatic spirituality a response to God is to say that as people become sensitive to their most productive emotions they learn to channel these emotions for more than personal or selfish purposes.

I agree with Phillip Rieff that charismatic spirituality moves people to affirm greater and greater responsibility—to take upon themselves new or renewed interdicts and obligations. I do not, however, think that this involves a self-conscious change of orientation or practice. No human being, I believe, exists without accepting such patterns of duty and self-restraint. What people need, I hold, is a reminder of what they have always been striving to achieve and a reassurance that they are moving in the right direction.

This work incorporates or adapts material I have previously published elsewhere. I acknowledge the permission given to use or adapt the following: "Prophecy, Ethics, and Social Involvement: Moses Maimonides, Baruch Spinoza, and Abraham Heschel," forthcoming in *Modern Judaism,* "Great American Jewish Thinkers and their Attitude towards Diaspora," *Encyclopedia of the Jewish Diaspora: Origins, Experiences, and Culture.* Volume 2: Countries, Regions, and Communities. M. Avrum Ehrlich, ed. (Santa Barbara, California: ABC-CLIO, 2009), 566-70. "Rethinkng Jewish Ritual: Toward an Eclectic Approach," *Arc: The Journal of the Faculty of Religious Studies, McGill University, Montreal, Canada* 27 (1999): 67-78, and "Franz Rosenzweig and the Development of Postmodern Jewish Ethics," *The Rosenzweig Yearbook 3: The Notion of Europe* (Freiburg: Verlag Karl Alber, 2008), 71-97.

The life of my mother-in-law, Esther Glick Gurian (1910-2008) exemplified what might be called charismatic spirituality.

While not a "traditional" Jew in the generally accepted meaning of that word, she led a life of awareness of rules and obligations, of duties and expectations. Not only in word and thought but by action with her family she showed an open acceptance of all people and of the general humanity we all share. I dedicate this book to her memory.

Abraham Heschel, Depth-Theology and Charismatic Spirituality

An Experiment in Depth-Theology

The Jewish theologian Abraham Joshua Heschel (1907-1972) was a religious leader active in social and political causes. He was ordained a rabbi within a mystical Jewish tradition that he never formally rejected. He has been understood as a religious moralist, as a symbol of Jewish spiritual life, and as an icon of contemporary Jewish religiousness. This study accepts such evaluations but finds them secondary to a different type of mystical power—that of the charismatic whose purpose is to challenge the status quo, to move people to a greater sense of responsibility, and to inspire a stricter adherence to the duties and obligations that come with being human.

Heschel's social and political concerns gained strength from his "religious insight" and the fact that he "held both God and human beings together in his thoughts at all times."[1] His wide range of theological and political thinking spanned specifically Jewish issues, general religious dilemmas, and the crisis of

---

[1] Susannah Heschel, "Introduction," in *Abraham Joshua Heschel, Moral Grandeur and Spiritual Audacity: Essays Edited by Susannah Heschel* (New York: Farrar, Straus, and Giroux, 1996), vii. Heschel's daughter is a scholar and ethicist in her own right; not only her personal experience with her father but her clarity of thought and cogent argumentation make her observations of utmost importance.

modernity as expressed in contemporary society.[2] Heschel addressed a wide audience of various religious and spiritual traditions. This ability to speak to a diverse constituency proved one of his great strengths.[3] The description cited above characteristically focuses on God and "human beings,"—not merely Jews or merely men, but all people.

This open concern reflects his theological stance. Heschel suggested that the modern situation calls for a new type of religious thinking, a type that he designated as "depth-theology."[4] Heschel claims that all religious groups, not merely Jews, face a crisis created by a culture of utilitarian thinking. In this culture, worth depends on usefulness. Comfort and success provide the criteria for value. In contrast to such a view, Heschel stood for communal responsibility, for a renewal of commitment to social causes, and a resurgence of spirituality.

In many ways Heschel exemplified the type of religious leader that Philip Rieff noted in what he himself saw as a "prophetic" response to the "triumph of the therapeutic."[5] Rieff,

---

[2] See the variety of essays included in the anthology mentioned in the previous footnote. The political concerns and their theological underpinning come out clearly in the section titled "Toward a Just Society," and the interfaith efforts in the section titled "No Religion is an Island."

[3] See ibid., viii.

[4] This is discussed in chapter one of this book. See also my article "Theology and Depth--Theology: A Heschel Distinction," *CCAR Journal* 21:3 (1974): 81--86.

[5] See Philip Rieff's introduction to the second edition of his *The Triumph of the Therapeutic: Uses of Faith After Freud* (Chicago: University of Chicago Press, 1966; second edition 1987), ix.

like Heschel, recognized the crisis modernity posed for people of faith. Like Heschel, he noted the collapse of social responsibility and civil concern. He located the origins of this crisis in what he called a "therapeutic" mentality that sought to release people from their repressions. He noted that while sublimation when done unconsciously takes instinctual needs and improves them, sublimation once recognized loses its force.[6] The loss of this power of improvement created a modern spiritual problem.

Religious leaders, however, seemed to him to supply a new type of communal power under which to subsume and restrain those instincts—social activism. The protests of the 1960s, especially the movement for civil rights, led him to a hope for a new culture of self-restraint and personal responsibility.[7] These movements used political causes as a means of reminding people of the importance of following rules, of exercising personal choice, and of deciding to channel their instincts in socially productive ways.

Rieff was ultimately disappointed in this hope, as his subsequent writings show. Perhaps the reason was that unlike Heschel, most social activists took the civil objectives as their main goal. Heschel differed from them in using the civil concerns as tools to awaken the spiritual life of individuals. As noted here in chapter one, Heschel contended that all the social issues had, at

---

[6] Ibid., 5--6.

[7] See Ibid., 18, 23, 240--1.

their root, problems of individual consciousness. Religions need to cultivate personal spirituality, using the symptoms of social ills as a point of departure. For Heschel, depth-theology represents a call for those personal changes for which society's problems are the symptoms.

This book addresses the same problem that Heschel and Rieff analyzed. It uses the stories and history of Jews as raw material out of which to derive those qualities necessary for a transformed personal spirituality. Like those who recognized the challenge of modernity, this book contends that both Jews and non-Jews face the same crisis. Both must work to sensitize a dulled human consciousness to spiritual values. In that way this book examines the substratum out of which any spirituality must grow but uses the sources of Judaism to uncover and illustrate that substratum. Abraham Joshua Heschel's example marks every chapter in this book, yet no chapter should be read only as an exposition of his work. Other scholars have refined the current understanding of Heschel. Raising the question of whether he is a "mystic" or an "ethicist" misses the point of the chapters that follow. These essays seek to build on Heschel's insights and develop some ideas of what might constitute the common elements of spirituality that all share.

Heschel's understanding of depth-theology provides a framework for the investigation that follows. Heschel represented a type of charismatic spirituality that worked back from Judaism to the roots of the religious impulse. He intimated but did not develop the particular virtues that underlie that impulse and give rise to spirituality. Each chapter of this book reviews Heschel's insight and continues by developing it into a discussion of one out of four basic virtues necessary for spirituality, generally understood—a responsive personality, compassion, generosity, and a skeptical view of civilization. In this way it follows Heschel's lead and then extrapolates some exemplary lessons. This experiment in depth-theology does not intend to be all inclusive or exclusive. The four virtues discussed here may be augmented by others. The point of the exercise is to suggest the contemporary value of moving from the particular and parochial interests of a single religious tradition to discover lessons for all.

What Is Jewish Religion?

This book explores different expressions of Jewish religion and the principles of spirituality associated with it. Common sense suggests that such an entity as "Jewish religion" exists. Jews practice something they call their "religion." The religion of "Judaism" is often placed together with the religions of Christianity and Islam as "Abrahamic religions." Nevertheless, modern scholarship often suggests that the term is misleading. Some Jewish and non-Jewish thinkers argue that "religion" has no place, either among Jews or among other groups. Wilfred Cantwell Smith once declared the "end of religion," claiming that the term no longer served a useful purpose. He remarked that because "The word 'religion' has had many meanings; it too would be better dropped." The variety of human activities associated with the term would be better studied on their own. The term obscures differences and pretends to a unity that is misleading. The words describing different religions-- "Judaism," "Christianity", or "Buddhism," for example-- are equally suspect.

Smith notes that while Jews may fight for "Jewishness" the idea of a "Judaism" arose only as Christianity sought to define itself in contrast to the culture of its origins.[8]

This book eschews any substantive definition of terms such as "mysticism", "spirituality", "religion" or "Judaism." Instead it draws inspiration from tales that Jews have told and experiences associated with the history they have encountered. Such an approach evokes the way Jews have understood themselves in relationship to other Jews, to non-Jews, and to the general environments in which they have lived. Jews have imagined the heroes of their past and projected those heroes into their present. They have created narratives expressing their relationships with others in both the past and present and used those narratives to inculcate certain virtues and attitudes toward the world. This book takes those tales and analyzes their implications for a spiritual life.

Charismatic Spirituality and Postmodern Jewish Religiousness

The meaning of the term "spirituality" challenges even those who are scholars in the subject.[9] Because any definition begins with the scholar looking inward, seeking confirmation of a personal experience in an external expression, different scholars

---

[8] See Wilfred Cantwell Smith, *The Meaning and End of Religion* (New York: Macmillan, 1962), 193--5; 71--3.

[9] See Mary Frolich, "Spiritual Discipline, Discipline of Spirituality: Revisiting Questions of Definition and Method," *Spiritus* 1(2001): 65--78.

derive different definitions of spirituality.[10] Understanding spirituality, however, requires more than just inwardness. It also entails looking outward, challenging personal experience through dialogue with others. Those others may interpret the same phenomena differently.[11] This study looks at both Jewish and non-Jewish views of spirituality to discover some common ground.

Philip Rieff introduced the dichotomy of the "charismatic" and the "therapeutic."[12] For Rieff the therapeutic seeks to resolve the tensions and ambiguities of life by releasing people from restraints and obligations. It considers interdicts and prohibitions as "inhibitions" obstructing personal growth. The charismatic, on the other hand, enables personal development precisely by reminding people of their duties, by imposing new regulations and rules. The key here, I believe, should be the term "reminding." People actually do live by self-restriction, but they need to recall the basis of their actions. Charismatic spirituality occurs as a mental shift from ordinary self-centered perspectives to a view that looks at the dynamics behind what appear to be trivial actions.

Such a charismatic approach to reality moves beyond the normative limitations to human experience. It demands that

---

[10] Ibid., 73.

[11] Ibid., 76.

[12] See Philip Rieff, *Charisma: The Gift of Grace and How It Has Been Taken Away from Us* (New York: Pantheon Books, 2007), 5.

people transcend ordinary convention to discover a higher responsibility. This sense of charisma corresponds to what Eugene Borowitz called "our postmodern spirituality." For several decades scholars have noted an increased concern with spirituality among Jews. Borowitz associates that spirituality with the Hebrew term *Tikkun Olam*, the repair of the world. Used in this way, spirituality is ethical. He suggests that this reveals a "paradoxical spiritual situation" in which Jewish identity evokes a recognition of a universal task, a duty to the world at large.[13] Borowitz notes that this experience of a oneness that transcends but also includes particular identity has surprised modern Jews.

These Jews have undergone a "spirituality that brings the self beyond itself" in contrast to the utilitarianism associated with modernity. He interprets this reality as a shock to modernists.[14] This postmodern spirituality may, Borowitz admits, be different than that of his father, but it continues a tradition and, therefore, remains within the framework of Judaism.[15]

That postmodern spirituality provides an example of what Rieff considers the charismatic. Jewish spirituality, as Borowitz understands it, illustrates how discontent with the status quo may lead not to a therapeutic rejection of all norms but to the

---

[13] Eugene B. Borowitz, *Renewing the Covenant: A Theology For the Postmodern Jew* (Philadelphia: Jewish Publication Society, 1991), 51.

[14] Ibid., 89.

[15] Idem., "My Father's Spirituality and Mine." in his *Judaism After Modernity: Papers From a Decade of Fruition* (Lanham: University Press of America, 1999), 7--18.

establishing of new norms. The ethical thrust that he associates with spirituality asserts new demands and expectations that surpass convention. Spirituality, as renewed responsibility, requires more of human beings than common ethics, it requires an extraordinary ethical concern. By remembering that concern, people may not change what they do, but will change their attitude to what they do.

In this way, Borowitz offers an alternative to the spirituality that Abraham Heschel once criticized. Heschel asserted that the human responsibility to God could not be fulfilled by what he called episodes of "spiritual rhapsody" or "excursions into spirituality."[16] Heschel opposed this type of spirituality to ethical sensitivity, to awareness of God's demands for moral actions. Heschel makes his comments, significantly enough, in what he calls a "philosophy of religion," not a philosophy of Judaism. He recognized that modernity challenged all contemporary human beings, not merely Jews. He turned to Jewish sources as a way of pointing out charismatic spirituality as a generally human possibility.

This book takes Heschel's approach as a point of departure, and, therefore, is less a depth-analysis of his thinking than the use of his inspiration to derive new approaches to ethics. The sources of Judaism become a means to recall humanity to its spiritual opportunities. In order to make use of those opportunities, people need to cultivate certain virtues. Those virtues, while illuminated

---

[16] Abraham Joshua Heschel, *Man is Not Alone: A Philosophy of Religion* (New York: Farrar, Straus and Giroux, 1951), 289.

by Jewish stories and history, are common to all human beings. This book, no less than Heschel's own theology, seeks to mobilize all people to activate spiritual virtues. By cultivating certain attitudes and behaviors, people become more prone to charismatic spirituality, more able to fulfill the ethical demands that transcend conventionality. This book shows how Jews have communicated those attitudes and behaviors.

The Perils and Possibilities of Universalism

The universalism implied by using Jewish sources to discover the roots of generally human spirituality may have a dangerous consequence. Models or paradigms, each true enough as a partial glimpse of reality, become in the hands of some investigators the single key to unlock every door. The Israeli scholar of the Kabbalah, Joseph Dan, for example, reports that he once met a Jungian scholar who was quick to point out to him that the cosmic vision portrayed in the kabbalistic book, *Sefer Yetzira*, in fact resembled a Jungian mandala.[17] The mystical work, on such a reading, becomes but one expression of a universal paradigm, a Jewish version of a psychological truth common to all human beings.

There is much in that book to confirm such an impression. The book takes as its presupposition the magical properties of the alphabet, of the human body, and of other aspects of the human and natural world. It would be strange if these elements, common to all human experience, could not fit into a Jungian pattern.

---

[17] Joseph Dan, *On Sanctity: Religion, Ethics and Mysticism in Judaism and Other Religions* [Hebrew] (Jerusalem: Magnes Press, 1997), 162--3.

10

Nevertheless, the specific problems of dating *Sefer Yetzira*, of determining its provenance, its place in the history of Jewish mystical speculation, and its relationship to non-Jewish mystical works, remain unresolved by applying such a Jungian panacea. A more profitable approach would be to use the Jungian model as one of several equally illuminating ways of discovering the varied dimensions of that mystical text.

The analysis that follows seeks to avoid the pitfall of overgeneralization by stressing diversity and difference. No single category exhausts the meaning of any virtue, story, or historical memory. The illustrations used serve to highlight how Jews have cultivated a type of charismatic spirituality and the roots of that spirituality. Certainly both that spirituality and its roots have significance for human beings generally. The specific examples do more than just point to Jewish experience, but they also resist reduction to a single meaning and significance.

Stories and Spirituality

Stories have played a crucial role in transmitting Jewish religious values. They stimulate religious impulses as well as give concrete models to follow.[18] The most important part of religious living, according to some Jewish thinkers, is finding the innermost point within oneself. Stories help achieve a recognition of that point.[19] The supernal secrets of religious devotion are

---

[18] See the discussion throughout Yitzhak Israel Buxbaum, *Storytelling and Spirituality in Judaism* (Northvale, NJ: Jason Aronson, 1994).

[19] Ibid., 14.

11

often considered too exalted for ordinary people to attain. The vision Ezekiel receives of the heavenly spheres confounds most intellects. A few mystical experts can study these secrets and glean their mysteries. Common people, however, do have access to the same spiritual insights. While the mystics imitate the supernal beings, ordinary people can imitate those mystics. The key to religious living, on this understanding, lies in stories about the mystical heroes.[20]

This present work makes use of stories for their "underlying purpose" which is not only to transmit ideas but to inspire that faith which leads to an acceptance of duties and responsibilities.[21] The stories told here are found in several different sources (with references given in the footnotes). Many of them are familiar, ancient, and often repeated. That repetition makes them more, not less, suitable here. It is told of Rabbi Hayim Tzvi Eisenbach that he would often retell stories again and again. Once a disciple questioned him about this, stating that he had heard one story just the day before. The rabbi replied with a question—asking the disciple whether he had prayed today. When the disciple admitted that he had, the rabbi continued by asking whether he had prayed yesterday as well. On receiving an affirmative answer, the rabbi commented that stories too needed to be repeated daily.[22]

---

[20] Ibid.

[21] Ibid., 141.

[22] Ibid., 110.

This tale teaches two important points. The first is the necessity for repetition—stories like prayers gain from being used again and again. Secondly, stories no less than prayers have the purpose of stimulating spirituality, of bringing the interdicts and obligations of religious life to consciousness. Since people change from day to day, so too the meaning and significance of the tales they hear change as well. Stories that take on different guises depending on their locale serve as reminders of the universal religious impulses underlying diverse religious expressions. Just as we follow daily routines such as those of hygiene or ritual expression, so too the routine of a familiar round of stories reinforces the common concerns that shape our lives.

Finally, stories represent some of the most universal elements in human culture. Very few stories are "original." Hasidic stories, for example, draw from many sources. Even as secular a text as that of Giovanni Boccaccio's *Decameron* serves as the basis for a tale told by the putative founder of Polish Hasidism, Rabbi Israel Baal Shem Tov, (often abbreviated as BESHT).[23] Such borrowing occurs often. The omnipresence of certain narrative motives suggests common spiritual concerns among human beings.

Perhaps the most common of all themes is that of children who have been lost or abandoned and only eventually after great difficulty either return home or discover their true parentage. Samuel Dresner makes two points about this motif—the first is that it sometimes becomes "the most important image" in Hasidic

---

[23] Ibid., 30.

tales and secondly, that while it might seem an appropriate parable for the experience of the Jewish people as a whole it is restricted to the experience of each individual person and may well be applicable to all human beings.[24]

Stories may seem to address a specific audience of Jews or Christians or Muslims or Buddhists. Instead they serve a universal purpose—that of reminding those in an audience of their hidden identity, of bringing to consciousness that charismatic spirituality that affords people a reaffirmation of those restrictions and duties that make them more fully human. Using stories such as these has a double purpose—it reminds Jews of their common humanity while reminding humanity of how Jews share in the general human condition.

An Example of Charismatic Spirituality and Its Meanings

The early modern Hebrew author, S. Y. Agnon, tells a tale that seems to be an affirmation of tradition. It seems to affirm the particularistic prohibition against intermarriage between Jew and · Non-Jew. When looked at carefully, however, it suggests the need to go beyond conventional rules and regulations. His tale "*Ve Lo Nikashel*," "So that we may not stumble," takes several unanticipated turns.[25] Agnon begins the tale by remarking that a

---

[24] See Samuel H. Dresner, *The Zaddik: The Doctrine of the Zzaddik According to the Writings of Rabbi Yaakov Yosef of Polnoy* (London: Abelard--Schuman, 1960), 177--9 and the comment on the use of this motif in Hasidism on.page 291.

[25] Shmuel Yosef Agnon, *Kol Kitvei S.Y.Agnon* , Volume II: *Elu veElu* [Hebrew] (Tel Aviv: Schocken, 1968), 289--95.

person should never change from an ancestral way of worship. Every tribe among the Israelites, he notes following a mystical tradition, originally had its own special *nusach* or variant liturgical form. In modern times, however, all has become confused, and the confusion among humanity has caused a confusion on high in the spiritual world as well.

In such a situation, Agnon continues, he no longer carries out his ancestral form of worship but instead seeks out all the diverse and variant versions he can find. This already suggests that scholarship, study and learning, investigating texts of the past, may provide a key to returning the world to its original perfection. Agnon abandons the traditional laws and restrictions on Jewish usage. In their place he puts a new set of expectations—those of eclectic scholarship. He has moved from one covenantal agreement to another. Rather than allow modernity to grant him a therapeutic release from rules and regulations he has discovered another more rigorous set.

When settling in the Land of Israel Agnon comments that he decided to live in Yaffo since it was a metropolitan center with a cosmopolitan population. There he discovered several synagogues of which even every separate Sephardic congregation had its own variation of the liturgy. In order not to be a "bad neighbor" (about whom the rabbis warn us to beware) he frequented different synagogues. Sometimes he would pray with one synagogue and sometimes with another, and even though he knew the prohibition against changing one's ancestral way of prayer, still he could not resist moving from one congregation to another and had become used to using a variety of liturgical

15

forms. Intellectual curiosity overpowered the force of traditionalism and its strictures. Agnon puts it bluntly, "Because I enjoyed diverse prayers, I permitted myself to change my liturgical forms." Here again charismatic spirituality moves him beyond ordinary restrictions and places even greater duties and responsibilities upon him. Agnon's experience with the variety of Jewish forms of worship parallels that of many non-Jews— Christians and Muslims included—who have learned to accept the diversity of traditions within their religious communities.[26]

When, according to the law of the freed slave as Agnon puts it, he was forced to leave Israel after seven years, he traveled throughout Ashkenazic lands and found that variant forms of the liturgy had proliferated in Europe. There he followed the ruling that you should use the "custom of the place," and once again encountered a variety of liturgical versions. Nevertheless, there was one liturgical variant he never changed—the blessing recited after meals. He had inherited from his ancestors a peculiar version of the paragraph seeking divine mercy.

As most prayer books render it, the prayer concludes by asking "Let us not be shamed nor disgraced forever." Agnon's version added an additional petition "And let us not stumble," "Ve Lo Nikashel," a variant on that prayer corresponding to a

---

[26] I cannot help but be reminded here of how the actress Judi Dench decided upon a place for a funeral of her husband Michael. She declares "Our churchgoing had always been very ecumenical: Michael went to Mass and I went to my Quaker Meeting, but we often attended our local Anglican church together, so that was where we held the funeral, with four priests sharing the prayers." Judi Dench (as told to John Miller), *And Furthermore* (New York: St. Martin's Press, 2010), 201.

similar variant found in the second blessing before the recitation of the morning *Shema*. That variant he never changed even though he found no other liturgical version that reproduced it.

Here it appears that Agnon has abandoned his charismatic spirituality to reaffirm a more traditional liturgical form. Nevertheless, here too he actually asserts a spirituality beyond the conventional. He accepts, once again the greater responsibility of diversity by adapting to the customs of various places. He had, however, one responsibility that transcended even this one—that of preserving the special legacy of his own family. That legacy represented a charismatic spirituality of its own, a unique liturgical obligation that apparently had no precedent.

Once, after he had returned to Israel, he hosted a visitor, a young girl from a good Jewish family who, on hearing him recite the grace after meals, questioned him about his version of the prayer. She claimed that no prayer book of which she knew mentioned that variant. He tried to disprove her claim, but could not find evidence of the validity of his version. After she left Israel to complete her academic studies in Europe she sent Agnon a copy of her doctoral dissertation that had focused on the variety of customs and liturgical forms. Agnon suggests that he was not fully pleased with her work, but delayed writing back to her.

At the yearly anniversary of the death of Agnon's father, Agnon knew that he would be called upon to lead the worship. Because he changed liturgies so often, he wanted to find a book that would guide him in this particular synagogue. He went to buy a prayer book for this purpose, and there in the bookstore he found a small book with the words of the grace after meals

17

printed on it. That text included just the words that Agnon's father had used, the variant that the new Ph.D. had claimed did not exist. He purchased the book and sent it and highlighted the contested words of the prayer "And do not let us stumble." Sometime later the girl wrote back that she was returning to Israel so she could get married in Jerusalem and invited him to the wedding.

At the wedding the bride showed Agnon what she had done with the small prayer book he had sent her. It was now bound with precious leather and adorned with jewels. He remarked that this was putting a book worth a penny into a case worth far much more. She explained that this book had been a turning point in her life. She had been about to marry a Non-Jew when the gift had arrived. The prayer not to stumble seemed, she thought, addressed directly to her. Because of that warning she called off her marriage to the Non-Jew and eventually married her childhood friend. Her marriage, she claimed, was a miracle caused by the arrival of Agnon's prayer book.

This story has several intersecting and apparently contradictory themes. On the one hand fidelity to the past is emphasized. Loyalty to in-group solidarity triumphs in the end. Yet the road to that solidarity is a circuitous one. Agnon himself is able to find the correct prayer book only because he had no set liturgy of his own but moved from one tradition to another. The girl who studied Jewish customs was ready to be moved by Agnon's gift because she had involved herself in the study of Jewish sources. Had she not roamed far afield she might not have been tempted to intermarriage, but at the same time she would not have been ready to receive the gift sent to her.

Whether we accept the premise that intermarriage would have been an act of disloyalty or not, what is clear is that the girl's spiritual transformation took place because she saw in study and learning something more than a means of receiving a Ph.D.; it also constituted a way to listen to cryptic messages addressed to her inner life. The story suggests that Agnon himself would not have discovered the liturgical validation he sought had he not engaged in charismatic spirituality. The girl as well could not have received his discovery and allowed it to change her life had she not been willing to see more than a mere curiosity in what she studied.

The double lesson here applies not just to Jews but to all people. The first lesson is that piety must expand beyond mere tradition. Whether diversity in and of itself becomes a virtue or whether unique familial variations create a new type of spiritual disciple, piety requires the infusion of the new or different. The second lesson is that study should never be an end in itself. Learning and education should point to transformations of the self. One question, never answered here, remains. What inspired both Agnon and his young guest to discover charismatic spirituality? The very process of study, learning, and the gleaning of more information seems to lie at the basis of the transformation. The point of education may well be the inculcation of a method of thinking, a way of questioning and sensing challenges rather than in any specific agenda, set of facts, or curriculum. Modernity challenges religious people of all traditions to discover the roots of the openness to the charismatic rather than the therapeutic that the protagonists here display. This book, like Agnon's story, does not explicitly advocate any particular action. If actions follow, it is because they flow from the nature of the individual involved and the experiences that shape that individual's life. Events arise from reminders, not from explicit norms.

The Course of This Book

This book examines the question of what makes the type of charismatic spirituality found in Agnon's tale possible. The first chapter provides the basic approach used in this book. It begins with a general exploration of how religions interact with one another and how Heschel's idea of depth-theology applies to that interaction. The chapter examines both the ecumenical context that makes possible the sharing of Jewish spirituality and the precedents in Jewish thought underlying such a sharing. The second chapter takes seriously Heschel's injunction to look to the heavens and ask, as does the book of Isaiah, "Who created these?" Since this volume is not essentially a treatise on Heschel, this chapter begins not with his thought but with general considerations about the meaning of personality and human spirituality. Looking at stories of creation, as Heschel has suggested, does indeed aid in understanding the basis of a spiritual, or if you will, mystical, self. Creation stories demonstrate the need for a responsive selfhood, an idea central to any spirituality. The next chapter focuses on what Heschel no less than James Joyce called the nightmare of history. It insists that recognizing the tragedies of human experience evokes compassion. The third chapter takes seriously Jewish life in the Diaspora as an example of cultural pluralism. Such a pluralistic legacy legitimates culture and the virtue of generosity it demands. Finally, Heschel's skepticism of "civilization," suggests not only disenchantment with modernity but also the reasons for the factionalism of Jewish religiosity from earliest to modern times. The final chapter of the book, a type of epilogue or coda, shows how the story of a Hasidic ritual, an innovation rather than a traditional rite, takes on different forms as it illustrates one or another of the four virtues that make up the central chapters. That chapter takes Heschel's striking criticism of ritual, ceremonies and symbolism as its starting point. Taken together these chapters provide one example of how an examination of Jewish sources can guide religious people of all traditions toward a more rigorous and creative spirituality.

CHAPTER ONE:

Charismatic Spirituality, Abraham Joshua Heschel, and Depth-Theology

Depth-Theology and Religious Spirituality

What metaphor best describes the relationship of one religion to another? Martin Buber claims that each religion is a "house" to itself, but a house with windows. Different religions call to each other, each out of its own window.[27] In contrast one might suggest that religious people interact with one another in a general place of meeting. Every particular religion is a passageway leading into "either the common reality of universal faith or the common marketplace in which a productive exchange of views is the basis of social creativity."[28]

Another metaphor may be even more apt. The houses of religion may surround a common courtyard. Believers mingle in that courtyard and share stories with one another. From those stories they glean what is common to them all and learn how to recognize themselves in others and others in themselves.

Abraham Joshua Heschel thought of religions in this way when developing his idea of depth-theology.[29] Depth-Theology

---

[27] See Martin M. Buber, *A Believing Humanism: Gleanings*. tr. with an introduction by Maurice Friedman (New York: Simon and Schuster, 1955), 115.

[28] S. Daniel Breslauer, *The Ecumenical Perspective and the Modernization of Jewish Religion* (Missoula, MT: Scholars Press, 1978), 123.

[29] See my "Theology and Depth-Theology: A Heschel Distinction," *CCAR Journal* 21:3 (1974), 81--86.

23

seeks to discover the existential questions for which religion, or theology proper, offers potential answers. While religions differ in the answers they provide to those questions, and thus are divided from one another, they find common ground in the problems they address. Heschel advanced the idea of depth-theology as a response to contemporary social problems. He stressed that only cooperation among diverse religious groups could solve the underlying issues facing modern men and women.

That emphasis on general principles enabled him to span both Jewish and non-Jewish concerns. The Jewish tradition long held that non-Jews were subjected to the seven laws of Noah, laws that could be expanded to included all the laws Jews found in the Torah.[30] Thus Jews realized that they shared "religion" as such with all other human beings.

Heschel spoke to "religion" generally rather than to Jewish religion exclusively. He may be seen as "transgressing" the parochial boundaries of Jewish identity. Nevertheless, he did so · because he wished to initiate both modern people into a new order of commandments and prohibitions, or at least reintroduce them to an old order that they had abandoned. While he saw "religion" as an answer to human questions, he insisted that the primary task is recovering the one profound "question" to which it actually responds. Depth-Theology, as he explained it, looks at the foundational spiritual condition from which all particular

---

[30] See David Novak, *The Image of the Non--Jew in Judaism: an Historical and Constructive Study of the Noahide Laws* (New York : Edwin Mellen Press, 1983).

24

religious traditions spring.[31] Depth-Theology consists of those general principles that underlie religious thinking. Rather than seek Jewish precedents for fair housing, for liberal programs supporting the elderly, or even for withdrawing from a disastrous military engagement, Heschel points to broad ideas common to humanity as a whole.

Heschel argued that modern life demands a depth-theological focus.[32] Several specific social problems seemed to command his attention—the war in Viet Nam, the proliferation of atomic weapons, racism. Beyond these, however, he identified the greater problem as a lack of sensitivity. "Our greatest threat," he writes, "is callousness to the suffering of man." In a similar vein he argues that the war in Viet Nam is a "human emergency," an emergency of "human anguish," rather than a question of political policies.[33] He argues that while some may suffer from degradation through poverty, Americans suffer from degradation through power.[34] Heschel sought to restore a balanced perspective.

---

[31] See *The Insecurity of Freedom: Essays on Human Existence* (New York: Farrar Straus and Giroux, 1966), 115--26.

[32] See the variety of issues included in Abraham Joshua Heschel, *Moral Grandeur and Spiritual Audacity: Essays Edited by Susannah Heschel* (New York: Farrar, Straus, and Giroux, 1996).

[33] Heschel, *Insecurity.*, 58, 179.

[34] Heschel, *Man is Not Alone*, 104.

25

He saw his task as reminding Americans of their own insecurity, of their lack of humility, of the need for a spiritual renewal that arises from a sense of vulnerability and common human weakness. While Heschel titled his book *The Insecurity of Freedom*, it might better be titled "the freedom of insecurity." Human beings discover their freedom only through recognition of their weaknesses, only through seeing that they are as dependent on God as God depends on them. Recognizing common responsibility brings freedom. That responsibility corresponds to the needs each person fulfills—human needs but also divine ones[35] Heschel's focus on the general human condition arose from his diagnosis of the crisis brought on by modernity, a crisis that derives from a false sense of security, a false self-satisfaction with what humanity can achieve.

Heschel construed modernity as a trap, as a fallacy of self-sufficiency. "Modern man," he complained, "fell into the trap of believing that everything can be explained."[36] Heschel wrote in order to free people from that trap. Since the condition extends to all modern human beings, he addressed every human being. He created a dialogue between traditions because all religions face the same challenge—that of modern self-delusions. He

---

[35] See the study by Morton C. Fierman, "Some Thoughts on Freedom in the Theology of Abraham Joshua Heschel," *CCAR Journal* 23:3 (1976), 91--100. See also the excellent article by Robert McAfee Brown, "Some Are Guilty, All are Responsible: Heschel's Social Ethics," in John C. Merkle, *Abraham Joshua Heschel: Exploring His Life and Thought* (New York: Macmillan, 1985), 123--41.

[36] Heschel, *God In Search of Man: A Philosophy of Judaism* (New York: Farrar, Straus and Cudahy, 1955), 43.

researched the substratum out of which religion grew because modernity has, by obscuring that substratum, made all religions equally suspect.[37]

Heschel's unique approach that allowed him to bridge institutional boundaries stems from his recognition of the universal challenge raised by modernity, one that transcends traditional distinctions between one spiritual path and another. "Is it not true," he asked rhetorically, "that facing disaster together we must all unite...?" He assumed both in this question and throughout his writing that the answer must be "Yes, it is true." His commitment to depth-theology and to the general principles that he felt must bring all faiths together derives from this implied answer to the question of modernity.[38] Heschel stands not only as a theologian but also as a source for contemporary spirituality.

Stories and Charismatic Spirituality

Stories provide the best vehicle for addressing this contemporary need to revitalize spirituality. One story often cited in several contrasting contexts illustrates this point.[39] The story

---

[37] Ibid., 7.

[38] Heschel, *Insecurity*, 180.

[39] The most often cited version of this tale is that in the Arabian Nights. See Jorge Luis Borges, "The Tale of Two Dreamers." In his *Collected Fictions*. Edward Hurley, tr. (New York: Penguin Books, 1999), 56--57, and Richard F. Burton, tr, *The Book of the Thousand Nights and a Night*. (London: The Burton Club, 1885), Vol. 4, 289--90. Paulo Coelho uses this tale as both the framework and basic theme of his *The Alchemist*. Alan R. Clarke, tr. (San Francisco:

tells how a once wealthy person, now fallen on hard times, laments his fall from fortune. His appeal for help is answered and he dreams that a supernatural voice tells him of a great treasure hidden in a distant city. When reaching that city, however, the protagonist discovers attainment of the treasure impossible because of guards preventing its recovery. When speaking to the guards, the protagonist learns that they have had a similar dream about a treasure on the very doorstep of the hero's home. The usual interpretation of the story is that one must leave home in order to learn what is important there. Jewish versions of this tale reinforce this view.[40]

The Jewish versions of the story, however, suggest a nuance not found in the original. These renditions of the tales do not mention a fall from wealth. They also emphasize the cultural difference between the poor man and the chief of police making the class distinction between the protagonists a major issue. While the original tale has the hero originally part of the wealthy class, the Jewish version makes the most of the hostility between

---

HarperSanFrancisco, 1993). The story itself may have a Jewish provenance as Burton's footnote shows explaining the origin of the word for supernatural "speaker" who comes in the dream as derived from a Hebrew source.

[40] See my use of the tale in my *Judaism and Civil Religion* (Atlanta, GA: Scholars Press, 1993), 23--26 and my *Creating a Judaism Without Religion: A Postmodern Jewish Possibility* (Lanham: University Press of America, 2001), 201--3, 218--9. See also Wendy Doniger, "The Love and Hate of Hinduism in the Work of Jewish Scholars," in *Between Jerusalem and Benares: Comparative Studies in Judaism and Hinduism*, Hananya Goodman, ed. (Albany: SUNY Press, 1994), 18.

rich and poor. The more usual variant[41] has the encounter one between a Jew and a Gentile. In one strange variant[42], the hero follows the advice of a mystical leader, the Baal Shem Tov, and then meets up with another Jew who, however, is a skeptic of this mystical master. Eventually this skeptical antagonist recognizes the truth in the hero's dream. The two become reconciled, and, emphasizing the theme of generous sharing, the treasure is split between the two protagonists.

Certain elements remain constant in Jewish versions of this classic narrative. In every case, meeting with someone outside of his normative experience provides the hero with the key to his treasure. The theme is not merely going to another place, but facing the discomfort of encountering the "other," a person who disconfirms the hero's life choices. The prominence of this story in so many versions suggests that as members of different groups hear the tale they see themselves in it. They recognize a message addressed specifically to them, even if told by another. That recognition provides a basis on which one religious tradition may speak to another. Stories like these show how members of one group can benefit from generously sharing with and learning from members of another.

---

[41] See Pinhas Sadeh, *Jewish Folktales Selected and Retold by Pinhas Sadeh*. Hillel Halkin, tr. (New York: Doubleday, 1989), 287, 383 and Mordekhai Ben--Yehezkiel, *Sefer Ha--Ma'Asiyot [Hebrew]*. Volume 6 (Tel Aviv: Devir, 1957), 22--29.

[42] Ben--Yehezkiel, *Sefer*, 36--44.

What is such a tale teaching? At its base the story advocates discomfort — the suffering that attaining any great reward entails. It goes beyond this general teaching, however, to introduce a more specific lesson. The most productive discomfort comes from crossing boundaries, following directives that seem to require a type of transgression, a type of transcending the ordinary limits of human experience. This human model exemplifies what might be called "charisma," a becoming informed by spiritual insight so as to create new demands, accept new responsibilities, and move in new directions.

The meaning of charisma used here follows the usage of Phillip Rieff.[43] Rieff contrasts charisma to what he calls "the therapeutic." In his view charisma sets out prohibitions (interdicts) while the therapeutic releases from all restraints. Charisma, whether conservative or radical, seeks to replace a failed system of laws and rules with one that stems from a truer or more authentic authority. Rieff focuses on prohibitions, but even his examples (such as the ten commandments and the teachings of the Hebrew prophets) include positive commandments as well as injunctions against actions. Rieff sees this as moral teaching, as activist preaching to change people's lives.

Another approach may see the prophets as uncovering the possibilities that lie within each person. They recalled their audience to the choices already made, to commitments beyond the conventional ones they thought adequate. The spirituality

---

[43] See Phillip Rieff, *Charisma: The Gift of Grace and How It Has Been Taken Away from Us* (New York: Pantheon Books, 2007).

found in religious stories arises when believers transcend one system of authority and regulation and enter into another, presumably "higher" or more godly than the former.

This higher authority stems not from some "new" revelation but from a reminder of obligations and expectations that came before the conventional authority became standard. The stories and laws derived from different places and historical periods naturally use diverse vocabularies, heroic figures, and forms of expression. Nevertheless, they contain a single unifying theme—that of going beyond the boundaries of what had been considered the ultimate authority and reaffirming a transcending authority in its place.

Aggadah, Halakhah, and Jewish Spirituality

The emphasis on stories such as that of the buried treasure corresponds to the rabbinic category of aggadah in contrast to the category of halakhah. Scholars define the difference between the two ways of expressing Jewish religious thought in many ways.[44]

---

[44] I provide a review of the discussion in my *Toward a Jewish (M)Orality: Speaking of a Postmodern Jewish Ethics* (Westport, CT: Greenwood Press, 1998), 25--30 and a discussion of the essential nature of *halakhah* for Jewish ethics, 63--77. Among the sources cited are Leo Baeck, *This People Israel: The Meaning of Jewish Existence* Trans Albert H. Friedlander (New York: Holt, Rinehart and Winston, 1964), 208--9, Judah Goldin, "The Freedom and Restraint of the Haggadah," in his *Studies in Midrash and Related Literature*, Barry L. Eichler and Jeffrey H. Tigay, eds., (Philadelphia: Jewish Publication Society, 1988), 253--69. , and Emmanuel Levinas, *Nine Talmudic Readings*. Annette Aronowicz, tr. (Bloomington: Indiana University Press, 1994). Although focused on both the essays and poetry of Hayyim Nahman Bialik, the study by Zipora Kagan, *Halacha and Aggada as a Code of Literature* [Hebrew] (Jerusalem: Bialik Institute, 1988) offers insight into both Jewish law and lore generally. See also the discussion of Eugene Borowitz on why theology tends to be aggadic rather than halakhic in his

31

At its most elementary level, the distinction is between legal material and attitudinal teachings. Law regulates behavior in very specific terms. Stories and lore, however, provide the basic principles on which the law is based. Halakhah is essential for any lived experience of Jewish religious life. It regulates those deeds by which people transform ideals into actual practice. Aggadah, however, provides the basis on which such a transformation takes place. It provides an ethics of general goals and values by which to evaluate what must be performed in any specific situation.

Tradition affirms that both are necessary and that competition between them leads to disaster. Judah Goldin cites the story told in Talmud Baba Kamma 60b in which a rabbi is forced into silence because of that competition. The rabbi compares the situation to that of a man with two wives, one older and one younger. The former pulls out his black hairs so he will be left gray; the latter pulls out his gray hair so he will be left only with dark hair. He ends up bald.[45] The two forms of rabbinic expression interact closely, as Jose Faur points out. A Halkahkic decision may well point to the principle it exemplifies. An expression of principles may enumerate the legal expectations it implies. In this vein, Faur notes that Jewish laws restricting contact between Jews and Christians legitimate themselves by

---

How Can a Jew Speak of Faith Today? (Philadelphia: Westminster, 1969), 19--20 and in his *Renewing the Covenant: A Theology For the Postmodern Jew* (Philadelphia: Jewish Publication Society, 1991), 57.

[45] I develop this story at greater length in *Toward a Jewish (M)Orality*, 17.

reference to an aggadic teaching that the putative ancestors of the two groups—Esau and Jacob—were at odds with each other. He also notes that the seven laws said to have been revealed to and incumbent on all human communities stems from an aggadic reading of the biblical tale of Noah.[46]

That example, however, suggests an important difference in attitude toward non-Jews. Non-Jews, in general, are given a more favorable treatment in the aggadah than in the halakhah. The mystic aspect of Jewish teaching, the aggadic content of rabbinic Judaism, reaches out to universal ideals and values. This, perhaps, is its essential purpose. Richard Rubenstein asserts that what aggadah provides is "the gift of meaning." It enables rabbinic Jews to express repressed ideas, to act as a safety valve for potentially dangerous desires, and shapes the way people look at life.[47] The aggadah, then, uses a specifically Jewish technique to achieve a generally human aim—that of coping with the tensions and strains of living. Understood this way Jewish spirituality uses traditional law and lore to transcend the Judaic element within them. In this way Jewish spirituality takes the tools of various Jewish religious expressions to create a sense of the universally human aspirations for transcendence.

---

[46] See Jose Faur, *Golden Doves with Silver Dots: Semiotics and Textuality in Rabbinic Tradition* (Bloomington: Indiana University Press,1986), 89.

[47] See Richard L. Rubenstein, *The Religious Imagination: a Study in Psychoanalysis and Jewish Theology* (Boston: Beacon Press, 1968), 171--83, and throughout this provocative and insightful volume.

Abraham Heschel's View of Prophetic Spirituality

Heschel often stressed the importance of both halakhah and aggadah.[48] He once declared that "Halacha without agada is dead; agada without halacha is wild."[49] He insisted that the general concepts of aggadah always take the shape of and remain within the boundaries of Jewish law. Nevertheless, Heschel recognized that the central issue challenging modern Jews was not that of halakhah, but rather the question of meaning, the realm of significance devoted to the aggadah. He dedicated himself to awakening people to the reality of the divine and cited the rabbinic claim that "If you wish to know your Creator, then go to the aggadah since through it you will learn to act in His ways (Sifre 49).[50]

This citation brings up two important points. The first is that the teachings of the aggadah do indeed result in consequences for action. Aggadah teaches people how to imitate the divine; it inculcates deeds of *Imitatio Dei*. Secondly, while the theological ideas in the aggadah admit that God does indeed · have a parochial concern for the people of Israel, for Heschel, the key of the aggadah is God's aspect of creator.

---

[48] See Abraham Joshua Heschel, *Theology of Ancient Judaism* [Hebrew] (London: Soncino, 1962), x--xxxviii; *God In Search*, 326--7, 336--9; *Insecurity*, 216--19; *Mans Quest for God: Studies in Prayer and Symbolism* (New York: Charles Scribner's sons, 1954), 133--7

[49] Heschel, *God In Search of Man*, 337. This aphorism echoes the statement in Kant's *Critique of Pure Reason* that "Thoughts without content are empty, intuitions without concepts are blind."

[50] Heschel, *Theology of Ancient Judaism*, vi.

34

The need to recognize the reality of the creator extends beyond Jews to all human beings. Such belief represents one of the basic principles that Heschel identifies with depth-theology. Jewish moral writings divide into two types. The first focuses primarily on Jewish legal teachings, their specific ramifications and their general principles. Whether the concern evinced is for deriving specific directives in a very particularized case or drawing a more general conclusion based on specific directives, this approach makes the legal system itself, the system of *halakha*, central.[51] Jewish law defines the parameters of Jewish civilization, the contours of what is and is not permissible in social and personal life.

A second approach seeks to cultivate attitudes, to engender certain emotional responses, to define general principles for their own sake, as stimulants of moral sentiments or as motivation for correct behavior. Moralists such as the medieval thinker Bachya Ibn Pakuda, Hasidic teachers, or Musar leaders such as Israel Salanter stand in that tradition.[52] This approach looks as much to culture as to civilization, to the artistic, poetic, literary, and intellectual expressions that intimate human values, personal

---

[51] This is the dominant approach among Jewish ethicists today, whether traditionalists or modernists. See the discussion and bibliography in my *Toward a Jewish (M)Orality*; among the best practitioners of this approach are J. David Bleich, Eugene B. Borowitz, Elliot Dorff, Louis Newman, David Novak, and Byron Sherwin.

[52] See the study by Hillel Goldberg, *Israel Salanter: Text, Structure, Idea* (New York: KTAV, 1982).

commitments, and flights of imagination. Culture, unlike civilization, often valorizes the trespass of boundaries, the transcending of limitations.

Heschel's sympathies lay with the second approach, stressing "depth-theology" as a way to influence moral attitudes. Heschel expresses this spirituality as a legacy of the Jewish prophets (as does Rieff as well). His preoccupation with the biblical prophets lay less in a scholarly analysis of their historical or contextual background than in their responsiveness to ethical questions. For him, the prophets represented an exaggerated moral sensitivity. The prophets put into words an extreme response to the problems of society. They articulated the divine attitude that could brook no compromises or evasion from the errors of human behavior.[53] Heschel contrasted the age of the prophets to that of the Greek philosophers and to modernity. The prophets learned and expressed themselves in order to evoke reverence. The philosophical tradition wrote and learned in order to understand the world. Modernity encourages learning as a preliminary for usage.[54]

Heschel gave a modern voice to the pedagogy of the prophets—expressing outrage as a means of convincing an audience to discover reverence rather than usefulness in the world. In this sense Heschel was more than a moralist or ethical

---

[53] See the discussion throughout his *The Prophets* (Philadelphia: Jewish Publication Society, 1962).

[54] Heschel, *God in Search of Man*, 15, 34, 67.

commentator on contemporary life. He was a "mystic," that is a person discontent with the status quo because it falls below divine expectations. The prophets cried out against a world of callousness seeking to change it to allow the presence of charismatic spirituality. Expressing the emotional outpouring of prophetic spirituality reminds people of what they should already know; it arouses an awareness of the divine that every person experiences but often silences.

Even in one of his earliest writings, one explicitly focused on the "mystical element" in Judaism but one that exudes prophetic protest, Heschel insisted that the prophets had an inner sense of the "pathos of God," that they could participate in the emotions of the divine.[55] He reiterated that claim consistently, even when critics commented that attributing pathos to the divine was too close to Christian theology for comfort in a Jewish context.[56] More importantly, Heschel emphasized that the prophetic task entailed communicating that pathos to ordinary people. He claimed that the prophets achieved this task by stressing two basic ideas—the uniqueness of the divine and the "dynamics that prevail" between the human and the divine.[57] Prophetic sensitivity to the divine passion translated, for Heschel,

---

[55] Abraham Joshua Heschel, "The Mystical Element in Judaism," in *The Jews* II, Louis Finkelstein, ed. (Philadelphia: Jewish Publication Society of America, 1949), 620.

[56] See Eliezer Berkovitz, "Dr. A. J. Heschel's Theology of Pathos," *Tradition* 6:2 (1964), 67--104; reprinted in his *Major Themes in Modern Philosophies of Judaism* (New York: Ktav, 1974), 192--224.

[57] Heschel, "Mystical Element," 619.

into a demand to articulate God's pathos to the world at large. The purpose of being a prophet was not to experience the divine or even, although Heschel does stress this, to be experienced by the divine. The prophetic profession requires the prophet to transform the human world. The prophet's actual function "was to bring about righteousness in history, justice in society, piety in the people."[58] The prophet acted on the basis of charismatic spirituality—moving beyond ordinary boundaries and expectations so as to create a world in which divine demands could find an audience.

The Prophet As A Modern Model

Can the prophetic example offer a path to spirituality today? Certainly Philip Rieff thinks that the prophetic morality can. He notes that the prophets root their morality in an application of interdicts and commandments upon themselves. They are emblematic in their lives and in their bodies of the expectations they make of others.[59] This, he contends, arises from the institutions and structures that surround them, that enable them to stand not for an "extraordinary" spirituality, but rather a spirituality accessible to all.[60] His view of an "ordinary" charismatic spirituality emphasizes the need to remind people of their own potential.

---

[58] Heschel, *The Prophets*, 361.

[59] Rieff, *Charisma*, 41.

[60] Ibid., 45--52.

Heschel agrees with this goal. His writings seek to evoke in his readers the same common rather than extraordinary spirituality that the prophets gave to their audience. Nevertheless, he thinks that the modern condition makes this task particularly problematic. Heschel clearly fears that a secular, utilitarian modernity makes charismatic spirituality difficult. While he looks toward the Hebrew prophets, he also realizes that modernity creates special problems.

A well known Jewish tradition insists that prophecy ended with the end of the biblical period.[61] Some traditions insist that it was taken from the prophets and given to fools. Another tradition claims that prophecy was inherited by the sages who, although they did not receive the Holy Spirit would be worthy of it. The model here follows that of the story discussed in the final chapter of this present study—that of a ritual decline through the generations. Howard Schwartz notes this motif and suggests that prophecy has become a "kind of intuition" in which "the voice of God must be heard within oneself."[62] People today, however, need instruction so they can hear that voice. The spark of prophecy has passed from prophets through sages to storytellers who awaken human consciousness and awareness of a call addressed to them.

---

[61] See Howard Schwartz, *Tree of Souls: The Mythology of Judaism.* (New York: Oxford University Press, 2004), 18--20, for a discussion of that theme.

[62] Ibid., 19.

A tale tells about the Hasidic master Elimelech of Lizensk.[63] The rabbi was once immersed in the ritual bath together with others when he heard a voice telling him "Whoever helps such and such a saintly man who is being persecuted in such and such a town will be rewarded." He asked a neighboring person if he too had heard a voice. When receiving a negative reply, Elimelech decided that the call had been meant for him. He had a task to do—the rescuing of this saint. He thereupon went to the town and began preaching in public. The people were aroused by this preaching and repented of their treatment of the saint. They changed their behavior. Elimelech took his leave with a happy heart.

When leaving the city, Elimelech again heard a heavenly voice, this time granting him the power to bestow a blessing on any person of his choosing during the next twenty-four hours. He wondered to whom he should give this blessing, but then encountered a woman weeping in the field. She told him that she and her husband were poor and in distress, so Elimelech blessed her. From that time forward the couple prospered. During their prosperity they set up a charitable hostel and instructed the servants to give one gold coin to whomever asked, but if someone asked for more, they were to be brought to the couple themselves.

---

[63] See Micah Joseph Bin Gorion, *Mimekor Yisrael: Classical Jewish Folktales.* Emanuel bin Gorion, ed.; I.M.Lask, tr. (Bloomington: Indiana University Press, 1976), 985--6.

Once Elimelech was traveling the countryside seeking money to redeem some people who had been taken captive. He came to that town and went to the charitable hostel, and when he received one gold coin he asked for more since he sought funds in order to save lives. When he was brought to the couple, they praised heaven for having sent him to them again and explained that it was just such a chance that had inspired them to put this particular feature into play. They hailed him as Elijah the Prophet and sought to give him the entire amount that he said he needed. He refused saying that he was not Elijah the Prophet, but that he could see the blessing had been used well. He took only half the amount he needed telling the couple that others should attain merit from donating to the cause and that they needed funds to continue their charity.

This tale expresses several important points. Elimelech himself illustrates the value of heeding a prophetic voice heard within oneself. His response to the promptings he hears sets the story in motion. Secondly, the awakening of spiritual sensitivity occurs in two different ways. Certainly by his warnings and preaching Elimelech impresses an interdict on harming others and a commandment to honor saints upon his audience. One way to remind people of their duties through prophetic utterance is by teaching them obligations to fulfill.

The second part of the story, however, adds another element. Blessing others, enabling them to fulfill their dreams and hopes, also inspires charismatic spirituality on their part. By blessing the woman and her husband, Elimelech provided the basis on which they expressed their own sense of obligation and duty for charity. This too represents a prophetic task as their identification of Elimelech with the Prophet Elijah shows. Here an ordinary charismatic spirituality flourishes when given a chance. Finally the story implies that in this modern era prophetic influence works best if it is anonymous. Elimelech never tells others about the voice he has heard; he never reveals why he admonishes the people of the town nor why he blesses the woman. His explicit rejection of identification with Elijah reinforces this motif of hidden prophetic power.

The Universal Purpose of Modern Prophecy

The theme of anonymity leads into the type of universalism that Heschel advocates for modern believers. Heschel declared that "religious isolationism is a myth." The prophetic response found in the Hebrew Bible is common not just to Jews and Christians but to all religious souls that stand in "fear and trembling" where, he claims "all formulations and articulations" appear as "understatements."[64] The same motifs found in the story of Elimelech also occur in other tales concerned with non-Jews rather than with Jews.

One tale concerns a certain "Ali," a stereotypical Arab or Muslim name, who serves as the apprentice to a baker.[65] Ali's job entails keeping the oven stoked during the night. A certain rabbi lived near the baker's shop. At night, as he was studying holy

---

[64] Abraham Joshua Heschel, "From Mission to Dialogue," *Conservative Judaism* 21:3 (Spring 1967), 3, 7.

[65] See Sadeh, *Jewish Folktales*, 112--7.

books by candlelight, a wind blew out his candle. He went over to the baker's shop, and Ali relit the candle for him. This happened several times until Ali decided to come over to the rabbi's house and kindle the candle for him in his own study. When the lighting has been accomplished, the rabbi blessed Ali.

A series of unusual events follow in which Ali becomes wealthy and moves to Egypt where he establishes a reputation for charity and piety. Sometime after these events the rabbi who blessed him decides to go to the Land of Israel. On his way he stops in Egypt where Ali pays his stay at the inn and invites him to dinner. The rabbi worried about needing to eat nonkosher food, but felt he could not refuse his benefactor. He put aside his scruples (although wondering why God was giving him this test) and accepted the invitation. When he reached the dinner, however, Ali assured him that the food was kosher and cooked by his wife in accord with all the dietary laws. The rabbi was amazed, and Ali identified himself as the former baker's assistant and informed him that all his wealth was due to the rabbi. Thereafter the rabbi went up to Israel and every month received a stipend and food supplies from Ali enabling him to build a successful academy for Jewish study there.

As in the story of Elimelech, here too a blessing leads to acts of charity. A person's spiritual life changes because of the intervention of a holy person. Here too the spiritual nature of Ali lies dormant; he receives a blessing but no specific injunction; the blessing enables him to actualize a hidden potential. What makes this story especially significant, however, is the interaction of Jewish and Muslim sensitivities. The rabbi, without hesitation, gives a blessing to a Non-Jew. The Muslim recipient of the blessing, again without hesitation, supports the Judaic efforts of the rabbi and giving him the financial backing necessary to establish a place of Jewish learning. Both participants in the tale recognize that their obligations extend beyond their own community; both accept restrictions—Ali by following Jewish dietary laws and the rabbi by accepting the invitation even while thinking that he would be violating some Jewish prescriptions.

The key here lies in the sensitivity with which one human being treats another rather than in detailed religious legislation. That human connection transcends the details of law, dogma, or ritual that Heschel sees as a yoke that often "tends to violate rather than to nurture" the human spirit. The charismatic spirituality that leads to the type of response found in the story of Ali and the rabbi represents what Heschel designates "an altar upon which the fire of the soul may be kindled."[66] Depth-Theology uncovers such dormant qualities within all human beings.

Heschel considers the greatest threat to humanity the lack of such a fire in the soul. He looks to words of both blessing and warning to save the situation. He demands renewed "reverence for man," "indignation at acts of violence," and "burning compassion." By restoring those virtues he hopes to move people to a charismatic spirituality, an accepting of moral duties and responsibilities.[67] Heschel, as noted before, emphasizes aggadah.

---

[66] Heschel, *God In Search of Man*, 317

[67] Heschel, *Insecurity*, 180.

44

Nevertheless, he also claims that "law is what holds the world together," even if "love is what brings the world forward."[68] While he uses the language of story and lore, his intent is the transformation of action. He calls for a sensitivity that will both cultivate spirituality and enable the existence of spiritual teachers, those who inspire others to accept their responsibilities and duties. The way depth-theology reveals without haranguing the requirements for charismatic spirituality forms the basis of the following chapters.

---

[68] Abraham Joshua Heschel, *Mans Quest for God: Studies in Prayer and Symbolism* (New York: Charles Scribner's sons, 1954), 323.

CHAPTER TWO:

Heschel and the Spiritual Personality

Modernity and the Problem of Personhood

How does the crisis of religion in modernity intersect with the problem of personality development? Both share the same challenge—that of transcending the reductionism of a utilitarian mentality. The phenomenon of religion has been called one of the strongest arguments "to preserve the human personality" from scientific reductionism.[69] Personality and spirituality share a common dynamic—that of transcending the confines of a predetermined pattern. Just as people develop their unique personalities out of the complex of traits humans hold in common, so too do they develop spirituality out of the resources available to humanity. In this way, religion and spirituality provide individuals with the means to transcend the ordinary and create a spiritual identity. A charismatic spirituality reminds people that their potential goes beyond biological determinism.

Developments in modern technology have reduced human identity to biological and mechanistic proportions.[70] The self established by biometrics cannot change or grow—fingerprints,

---

[69] See Joachim Wach, *The Comparative Study of Religion*. Edited with an introduction by Joseph M. Kitagawa (New York: Columbia University Press, 1958), 12.

[70] See the discussion in Giorgio Agamben, "Identity Without the Person," in his *Nudities*. David Kishik and Stefan Pedatella, trs. (Stanford: Stanford University Press, 2011), 46--54.

the image of the retina, and other such features remain constant. Such consistency defies the reality of personal growth and change. The "person," or the mask by which people present themselves to others and through which they attain social confirmation alters from social encounter to social encounter. The demands upon the person alter as well. A static identity prevents the flexibility necessary for creating and maintaining a social self, a true personality. That type of fluid personality so challenged in today's world remains a necessity for charismatic spirituality.

The modern arresting of personality and spirituality at a single stage of development affects not merely the individual but also the social environment in which the individual lives. That unity surpasses any single "personality" type or model. A charismatic spirituality depends on the flexibility needed to allow a self to assimilate diverse influences and potencies. Both the community and the individual depend on people who, aware of their own inner diversity, respond creatively in the face of the different persons and challenges they face.

Jewish Spirituality and Human Personality

Jewish spirituality, as the previous chapter makes clear, requires individuals to go beyond a simplistic view of the self. Traditions such as those in Jewish religiousness enable people to do more than assemble an unrelated and disconnected collection of beliefs and practices from which to build their personalities and spirituality.[71] This recognition of the relationship between individual and social structures makes Jewish religion take the meaning of personality very seriously. Jewish community depends as much on a common view of human development as on a sense of history, culture, and civilization (each of these three are developed in later chapters).

Leon Stitskin sought to discover what is "Jewish" about Jewish philosophy. He concluded that one element consisted of a focus on human personality. He contends that Jewish thinking about religion and about the divine begins by probing not theology or natural science but the secrets of human existence.[72] Focusing on the development of personality suggests the injunctions and prohibitions demanded as a means of transcending mere instinctual living.

The aim of Jewish teaching, Stitskin claims, is " to attain an ethical personality, a spiritual personality, and a cognitive personality." The stories Jews tell reveal a means of achieving that aim.[73] That personality responds to diverse stimuli and demands. A fully realized personality is always in process, always becoming, moving flexibly from one aspect of life to another.

---

[71] See Sandra M. Schneiders, "Religion vs. Spirituality: A Contemporary Conundrum," *Spiritus* 3 (2003), 164--5; see the entire article, 163--85.

[72] See Leon D. Stitskin, *Eight Jewish Philosophers in the Tradition of Personalism* (Jerusalem: Feldheimn, 1979).

[73] Ibid., 21.

Abraham Joshua Heschel and the Human Personality

Abraham Joshua Heschel continued the tradition Stitskin describes but went beyond it to claim that the crisis of modernity affects all people today. He contended that the challenge of developing a dynamic and responsive self applied not to Jews alone but to everyone. Immanuel Kant, in the introduction to his "Lectures on Logic," avers that philosophy seeks to answer four basic questions: what can I know, what can I do, what can I hope for, and what is man.[74] Abraham Heschel not only rephrased the final question as "Who is Man?" but also saw only one question as crucial: how to remain an uncorrupted person in a world of lies. The necessity of being an authentic human being surpassed any intellectual queries that philosophers might pose.[75] Heschel insists that the crucial issue of personhood lies in the "moral deed," in decisions about living not for the self alone but for others. The essential nature of being human cannot be understood without such deeds or moral consciousness.[76] Human nature depends on responsiveness to a world of others, to moral consciousness and moral responsibility.

Heschel roots the responsible self both in human nature and in a view of divinity. He announces that responsiveness to others

---

[74] See Immanuel Kant, *Lectures on Logic*. J. Michael Young, tr. The Cambridge Edition of the Works of Immanuel Kant. (Cambridge: Cambridge University Press, 2004), 538.

[75] Abraham Joshua Heschel, *God In Search of Man: A Philosophy of Judaism* (New York: Farrar, Straus, and Cudahy, 1955), 179.

[76] Idem., *Who is Man?* (Stanford, CA: Stanford University Press, 1965), 36.

provides the foundation for both religion and morality. Both begin with the recognition that "something is asked of us." Human personality evolves in responsive to situations outside of the individual; it depends on answering the others who have need of us.[77] Heschel considers God's need of humanity the single most important element in the development of a personality.

Yet Heschel does not claim that human beings fulfill that need by a direct interaction with the divinity. God stands for the call for righteousness, the demand people feel upon them of the imperative to make the world more just.[78] God is the standard by which individuals measure the adequacy of their lives and their society. The more conscious they are of "God," that is of a rigorous ideal of righteousness, the more they dedicate themselves to changing reality.[79] All depends on the way human beings perceive themselves and their world. That perception enables them to act as partners to the divine.

The Unfinished Portion of the World

Heschel's view finds confirmation in Jewish lore. The rabbis argue that God intentionally left the world unfinished so

---

[77] Idem., *Man is Not Alone: A Philosophy of Religion* (New York: Farrar, Straus and Giroux, 1951), 215, 219--20.

[78] Heschel, *God in Search of Man*, 68.

[79] Heschel associates this insight with the teachings of Rabbi Menachem Mendel of Kotzk; see his *A Passion For Truth* (New York: Farrar, Straus and Giroux, 1973), 228--9.

that the creatures could complete it.[80] One version of this motif suggests that this unfinished corner of the world harbors the demons and devils of Hell. Hell is, therefore, not an original part of the creation of the world, but is rather an afterthought, created independently of the divine plan. Another view suggests that it is a place for sinful souls to hide from God. They need a refuge from the torments of the world, a safe haven in the midst of a chaotic world. Such a place of hidden safety suggests the importance of humility, the value of refraining from too much involvement in the world.

The dominant use of this motif, however, suggests that the world remains unfinished because humans must rise to the task of completing creation. By their actions humans make the world their own, they take possession of what had been a passive gift to them with their birth. The rabbis tell a story about a king who hired an architect to build him a palace. The architect created a beautiful structure but left one room unfinished. The king wanted to know why that room was bare. The architect answered that if he had finished everything the world would belong to him and not to the king. The king could make the palace his own only by putting his own mark upon it, by working on it himself. The world is like that. Human beings make the world their own only if they participate in its creation, only if the world evolves in response to its creatures.

---

[80] *Pirkei de--Rabbi Eliezer* 3; see the discussion of this motif and its various implications in Howard Schwartz, *Tree of Souls: The Mythology of Judaism.* (New York: Oxford University Press, 2004), 151, 213.

This complex of ideas concerning the unfinished nature of the world shows the way God as creator intimates the importance of human actions. The human mission involves active participation in constructing a better world. Humans must dare enough to add their ingenuity to the original work of the creator. They acquire this daring by remembering both their own powers of creativity and the inadequacies in the world around them.

The story applies the lesson taught by an incomplete world to all humanity not just to Jews. Every human being makes a unique contribution to finishing the work of creation. Every person plays a crucial world in improving the world. God's plan set the world in motion, but that plan continues to unfold. Only when human beings recognize their responsibility for furthering that plan do they function according to the divine design. God has not provided a ready-made reality that human beings should accept as a given. Instead the world as it is now offers a point of departure for further endeavors and creative actions.

The task of becoming a human being, Heschel claims, begins with the realization that nature in general, and human nature in particular, needs improvement. Religion, he insists, develops from the premise that human beings can surpass themselves, that every person can grow beyond what nature has given.[81] His view of personhood takes the story of the unfinished creation seriously as a point of departure for an investigation of piety.

---

[81] Heschel, *God in Search of Man*, 33, 399.

Heschel does not claim that human beings can understand God, only that they can become aware of the divine demand upon them. While philosophers may debate the nature of divinity, piety focuses instead on what God requires. Those requirements, Heschel insists, are not ambiguous.[82] God makes those divine needs explicit. How do people discover what God demands? One of the most significant and varied stories in Jewish narratives focuses on the act of divine creation. Creation myths do more than express either a construction of the world or an ethical presupposition. They may demand a response to that world.

Heschel recognizes this function in stories of creation. He cites the biblical verse (Isaiah 40:26) "Lift up your eyes on high and see: Who created these?" as indicating how consideration of creation leads to a new awareness of the divine and the meaning of the world.[83] He understands creation myths as fundamentally different from scientific explanations. Scientists, he avers, look at the world as a problem, as a puzzle to be resolved. The world is an "enigma" in need of a solution. Religious thinking, however, sees the world as an opportunity, a challenge calling forth a response. Creation understood from a religious perspective, he thinks, requires an answer. Facing a religious tale describing divine creativity, "All that is left to us is a choice–to answer or to refuse to answer."[84] Creation does not provide humanity with an

---

[82] Abraham Joshua Heschel, *Man's Quest for God: Studies in Prayer and Symbolism* (New York: Charles Scribner's sons, 1954), 124.

[83] Heschel, *God In Search of Man*, 31.

[84] Ibid, 111--2.

answer but rather with questions, with demands not a completed program.[85]

Heschel believes that if people look to creation they will discover the demands to which they must respond. Not only Jews but all human beings reside in the same created world, all people share in the same set of requirements that God sets before us. A person need not believe in a literal deity, an anthropomorphic figure who molds the world out of some raw material, in order to understand Heschel's point. He suggests that if we look closely at the world we have inherited we will discover certain duties and obligations addressed to us. He chooses to call the source of those expectations "God."

More importantly, however, he insists that all sensitive persons will recognize that they have tasks to perform merely by examining the world in which they live. It is in this sense that he declares "Responsibility is the essence of being a person, the essence of being human."[86] Discovering the clue to human personality, to selfhood, means first focusing on that which lies outside of the self, with examining the world of creation and the

---

[85] Heschel was certainly aware of the extended discussion of this passage in both the *Zohar* and the Introduction to the *Zohar* which culminates in the recognition that the Hebrew words "these" and "who" combine to make the divine name "elohim." See *The Zohar, Pritzker Edition.* Translation and commentary by Daniel C. Matt. (Stanford: Stanford University Press, 2004), 1--9.

[86] Abraham Joshua Heschel, *The Insecurity of Freedom: Essays on Human Existence* (New York: Farrar Straus and Giroux, 1966), 09; compare 130 where he declares the essence of being a self to consist of concern with other selves.

duties we have toward it. In Heschel's language this means responding to God's demands.

The Duality of Creation, Human Personality, and the Divine

Examining creation might well begin by looking at the biblical narratives of how the world came into being. The Bible, intriguingly, offers several conflicting views of that creative act. One example of that diversity is the difference between the stories of creation in Genesis 1:1-2:4a and in Genesis 2:4b-4:1. Genesis 1:1-2:4a tells one narrative concerning the creation of the world; and Genesis 2:4b-4:1 tells a very different one. The first seems to take a positive view of nature and the created world and the second a more negative one. The modern Jewish thinker Leo Strauss uses this duality in Genesis to suggest that the Bible recognizes the incoherence of any human speculation about creation.[87]

Heschel expounded a similar idea. He saw the creation story as an indication of the way human beings and the divine are "essentially different and incomparable entities." The tale was not meant to explain the world or make it intelligible. The point of such a story is to focus on what human beings must do about creation rather than how they should "understand" the Creator.[88]

---

[87] See the discussion by Leo Strauss, "On the Interpretation of Genesis," in his *Jewish Philosophy and the Crisis of Modernity: Essays and Lectures in Modern Jewish Thought* (Albany: SUNY Press, 1997), 359--76.

[88] Heschel, *God in Search of Man*, 15--16.

For Heschel, creation has at its base a set of demands made upon human beings.

Understanding the duties springing from the human relationship to creation begins with an acknowledgment of the diversity and variety of stories about it. The Jewish philosopher Moses Maimonides (1135-1204) makes the remarkable assertion "Know that our shunning the affirmation of the eternity of the world is not due to a text figuring in the Torah according to which the world has been produced in time." (Moreh Nevochim, II:25). Maimonides prefers an ethical justification of the belief (without it the Law would not be considered binding) because the texts describing creation are neither so numerous nor so univocal as to be definitive. One might say that this equivocal position on creation permits the variety of personalities essential in charismatic spirituality.

Rabbinic thinkers noticed the difference between the first two narratives in Genesis and drew moral conclusions from them. Rabbi Shimon ben Lakish interpreted this myth as suggesting two alternative views of humanity (Midrash Genesis Rabba 8:1): If one does well then they say "for you the world was created." If one does not do well then they say, "even the smallest insect was created before you." Human nature, like creation, is two-fold. Humanity can achieve much. The potential for human transcendence defines the goal and purpose of the individual. On the other hand, most people struggle just to overcome their wayward impulses. An individual alone cannot accomplish the task God sets. Only an individual armed with God's teaching, with Torah can achieve the ultimate purpose of human existence.

Jewish mythic narratives oscillate between these two views of human nature. Humanity as potential angel and spiritual being stands over against a view of humanity as straying and impulsive, in need of moral restrictions and detailed law.

A later thinker, the Hasidic Rabbi Simhah Bunam (d. 1827), made a cogent comment based on that difference as expressed in the midrash. "Every person," he declared, "needs two pockets. In one pocket should be the words "Even the smallest insect preceded me in God's thought." In the other should be the words, "All creation came into being for my sake."[89] Rabbi Bunam bases this claim on his reading of Genesis 1:1-2:4a and 2:4b-4:1. In the first story he notes that humanity comes into being only after the rest of the world has developed. This means that the creation of humans depends upon every other created being. In the second story he notes that after Adam has been created God brings forth creature after creature to see if it solves the problem of human loneliness.

Rabbi Bunam knows that these two portraits of reality seem to offer conflicting descriptions of creation. That contradiction does not bother him since he assumes that the stories are told to teach a lesson, to inculcate an attitude, rather than to describe the exact order in which creation took place. Rashi (the rabbi, commentator, and scholar Rabbi Solomon ben Isaac, 1040-1150, discussed at length in a following chapter) had already made that point explicitly in his commentary on Genesis 1:1—were the

---

[89] See Martin Buber, *Tales of the Hasidim: Later Masters* (New York: Schocken, 1947), 249--50.

58

description meant to portray the sequence of events at the beginning of time, he claims, the choice of language would have been different.[90]

More importantly, Bunam thinks, in contrast to Shimon ben Lakish, that the attitudinal lessons taught by each of the stories are complementary. Human beings sometimes need humility; they must restrain themselves in the face of temptations to transform the natural world. Humanity has a place within nature and should respect the dignity of other natural beings. Human beings, however, also need a type of daring and initiative. They improve nature, leaving it better than they found it. Bunam argues that certain situations demand human activity, human management of the world. The second story conveys this aspect of humanity's relationship to the world.

Bunam's point parallels that made by Walter Kaufmann in his exposition of what he calls the "four cardinal virtues."[91] Three of his virtues seem straightforward and easily understood— courage, honesty, and love. The fourth, however, requires more complicated discussion, the virtue he calls "humbition." For Kaufmann, humans should combine a humble sense of their limitations with an ambition to realize their talents and achieve apparently extraordinary goals. Either of these two qualities alone

---

[90] Rashi accentuates the political rather than the cosmological meaning of the passage—the Torah begins with a story of creation, he argues, to show that God had the right to give the land of Israel to the Jewish people.

[91] See Walter Kaufmann, *The Faith of a Heretic* (New York: Doubleday, 1961), 317--22.

may, he thinks, lead to an unbalanced character, one that is overly cautious or one that is overly risky. Combining them, however, creates a tension that leads to virtuous action.

This quality of humbition lies at the heart of the duality toward humanity's place in creation to which not only Rabbi Bunam's statement points but that also animate those duties to which humanity responds when interacting with the natural world. Those obligations consist in the apparently paradoxical call to be both humble and ambitious at the same time. Human beings, as Heschel realized, play a double role in the created world—reaffirming the intention of the creator and acting as a creative partner with the divine in making the world more perfect. Reminding people of the need for humbition also reminds them of the double potential within their personalities.

Humility and the Importance of Restraint

Genesis 1:1-2:4, usually thought to come from a late priestly source, suggests that humanity receives a commission to cultivate its image and become godlike. Such a view might seem to emphasize human power and ambition, nevertheless, a study of that story and its implications suggests the need for humility and restraint as people grapple with the world they have inherited. In that version, everything occurs according to a clear divine plan. God begins the creation by distinguishing between light and darkness. Each successive day brings a more complex division among created beings or a more complex set of creations.

The creation of human beings plays a distinctive role in this plan. Only humanity shares a common "likeness" with the creator and receives a peculiar directive: not merely to propagate itself

60

but also to serve as the rule or measure of everything else. God takes the initiative and creates humanity, male and female at the same time. Humanity is to the world what God is to creation: the symbol of its true purpose, the standard of natural life.

Genesis 1:26 and 28 use the Hebrew term "mashal" to describe the human task. Translators often render this as "have dominion over" but the word actually means to "measure" or to "keep within the rule of." Human beings are not to oppress the world or use it as a means to satisfy their whims. Instead they are to ensure that it follows the guidelines inherent in the original plan of creation.

This understanding of the human purpose leaves humanity with a responsibility–that of making sure that the world continues its natural processes. Human beings have the duty of keeping the divine pattern in place. The lesson of the story, then, is three-fold–to emphasize the goodness of the divine pattern inherent in the natural world, to valorize variety and difference in that pattern, and to place responsibility on human beings for the continuation and maintenance of that pattern. Such an evocative myth moves beyond the explanatory concerns of science to moral issues.[92]

The ethical implication of this emphasis on orderly evolution involves a trust in the created order, an acceptance of its changes and development, and a humility in the face of these

---

[92] See Benjamin Uffenheimer, "Myth and Reality in Ancient Israel," in *The Origins and Diversity of Axial Age Civilization.* Samuel N. Eisenstadt, ed. (Albany: State University of New York Press, 1986), 160--3.

processes. Human beings may be the caretakers of creation, but they must respect the dignity and inherent value of the natural world. Careless attempts to shape that world to fit selfish wishes and desires will only thwart the divine plan. Human beings should nourish and encourage the growth and development of the world that preceded them, but they should avoid interference in the orderly expression of the patterns infused into the world. This requires humans to learn restraint in their efforts to take charge of the world.

The Dangers of Lacking Restraint

When in 1967 Abraham Heschel considered how Jews and Christians might move from "mission" to "dialogue," he contended that people of faith should meet on the common ground of "humility and contrition." They should each recognize that their faith was insufficient, inadequate by itself, that aware of divine commandments, people should come together to answer a call for which they find themselves urgently lacking. He saw the necessity for interreligious cooperation grounded in an awareness of what each person could not accomplish separately.[93] Humility stands as a primary virtue derived from looking at the world as a created order.

Human beings often have a limited perspective on the natural world. They look at the immediate effect of some occurrence without taking a longer view. Storms, tornados, and earthquakes bring disaster to human habitations, nevertheless

---

[93] Abraham Joshua Heschel, "From Mission to Dialogue," *Conservative Judaism* XXI:3 (Spring 1967), 3--5; see the entire essay, 1--11.

they may be essential for keeping nature in balance. A story about King David illustrates this lack of perspective.[94] According to the story, the Babylonian king Nebuchadnezzar asked the Jewish sage Ben Sirah why God created such pests as hornets and spiders. Ben Sirah replied by noting that King David had asked the same question. David, in fact, went further than the king in defining the lack of usefulness involved—hornets, unlike bees, merely sting and do not produce honey; spiders spin but no one can wear what they spin.

God responded by telling him that he would eventually see their usefulness. The story then relates how, when King Saul sought to destroy David, he once hid in a cave. A spider came and wove a web across the mouth of the cave. Saul's soldiers came searching for David. When they noticed the spider's web, they ignored the cave thinking that if David had come that way, he would have broken it. In this way the spider saved David's life. On another occasion David crept into King Saul's tent while he lay sleeping. On his way out, however, he was caught between the sturdy legs of Abner who was guarding the King. A hornet came by, however, and stung Abner so that, without waking, the

---

[94] See Micah Joseph Bin Gorion, *Mimekor Yisrael: Classical Jewish Folktales* III. Emanuel bin Gorion, ed.; I.M.Lask, tr. (Bloomington: Indiana University Press, 1976), 106--7. Interestingly, Bin Gorion follows his sources and attributes the original query to Nebuchadnezzar, a non--Jewish ruler and only then mentions that David asks the same question. Hayyim Nahman Bialik in his *And it came to Pass; Legends and Stories about King David and King Solomon.* Herbert Danby, tr. With woodcuts by Howard Simon. (New York: Hebrew Publishing Company,1938), omits this reference and begins with the story of the king.

soldier moved his legs and freed David so he could escape. Thus David learned how useful these apparently useless pests could be.

The story suggests two reasons that humans should remain humble when judging the rest of creation. First, they never know what God's ultimate plan entails. They should trust that plan and not evaluate creation on the basis of their limited perspective. Secondly, if they wait patiently they will discover that what appears to be useless does in fact have a purpose that impacts their lives. It is best to use caution when seeking to remove so-called pests not only because of the limited perspectives humans possess, but also because in the long run humans as well as the rest of creation require these creatures.

Not only does human ignorance lead to a misjudgment of the value of natural creatures, it can also precipitate a disaster. Another tale of King David exemplifies this view.[95] This tale assumes that David rather than Solomon began the building of the Jerusalem Temple (this follows the discussion in I Chronicles 22 that contrasts with the narrative in I Kings 5-7). According to the story, David reached the foundation stone on which God had established the world. The stone shone like a great jewel, and David desired to see what lay underneath it. When he tried to do so a voice issued forth warning him that were the stone to be moved, the world would again be overwhelmed by a flood. David refused to listen to this warning. He had the stone removed, and

---

[95] See the discussion of this talmudic tale and its later ramifications in Schwartz, *Tree of Souls*, 96--7.

immediately the waters from beneath the earth began welling up and threatened to destroy the world.

David was perplexed. He knew that using God's secret name and inscribing it on the stone could stop the flow of water. He wondered whether such a use of the name would be justified. He sought counsel, and his chief advisor, Ahitophel, responded that God's name could be used to bring peace to the world. David thereupon engraved that name on the stone and stopped the waters. Solomon built the holiest part of his temple over that stone. He worried that some scholar could come, recite God's name, release the waters, and return the world to chaos. Stone lions were placed to guard the place and would roar when someone approached, causing them to forget the pronunciation of God's name.

This story shows how human arrogance and curiosity could threaten the existence of the world. Even in the presence of such a story about David, Solomon worried that scholars could still be tempted to interfere with the created order. Humility needed reinforcement from some other source—the roar of lions. This suggests the necessity of teaching people the humility necessary to protect the world from the human impulse to tinker with reality. The prohibition against interfering with the natural order even when unrestrained by specific rules and regulations represents a charismatic and spiritual program of living.

Heschel emphasizes human inadequacy, denying that its recognition depends not on "humility," he claims, but rather a fact of our existence. Both what people attempt and what they refrain from attempting fail to meet the standards of adequacy.

People must struggle against vanity and conceit.[96] Looking at the sweep of the natural world reminds people of their ignorance. Heschel characterizes such a view as fulfilling the rabbinic injunction to know before whom you stand. He uses the idea of divinity to remind people of their lack of complete understanding.[97] While this reference to a deity symbolizes human failings, people can sense the vastness of the world and their inability to comprehend it all without that reference. The virtue of humility by itself prepares people to discover new prohibitions on their interference with the natural order.

The Importance of Ambition

While humility prevents people from overstepping their boundaries, some situations require audacity. A person whose extreme humility (perhaps the type that Heschel denies in the citation above) leads to inaction may fail to achieve important goals. The Hasidic master Rabbi Mendel typified that type of humility. He refused to place himself in positions of responsibility. Once he attended a feast held by his master Rabbi Elimelech. Everyone had been given utensils at the feast except for him. The others ate the food with gusto while Rabbi Mendel remained quietly at his place, neither eating nor complaining.

Rabbi Elimelech turned to him and said, "One must learn to ask for a spoon."[98] Mendel took the lesson to heart. A student

---

[96] Heschel, *God In Search of Man*, 316, 407.

[97] Ibid., 407.

[98] Buber, *Later Masters*, 125.

must dare enough to ask questions, to demand the tools necessary for the task at hand, to engage in the efforts require to progress. Silence and humility may have their place, but each person has a role to play and a purpose to fulfill. Too great a focus on humility may thwart the necessary activism required of every individual.

Performing that task and purpose requires daring and persistence. A story is told of Rabbi Zusya who, no less than Rabbi Mendel, personified humility and self-effacement. According to this story he once asked his teacher, Rabbi Dov Baer, the Maggid of Meserich, to teach him the "ten principles of worship."[99] He probably expected an exposition of modes of prayer. Instead, the Maggid told him to learn three principles from a child and seven from a thief. Among these are those of screaming for what you want, applying yourself at night as well as during the day, trying again if you don't succeed at first.

These principles also appear in an earlier tale in which Dov Baer confronts a thief whom he had helped before. The thief apparently did not learn from his previous peril. The thief replied that even if he failed the first time he needed to try again. This type of persistence and daring contrasts with the humility urged by the normative tradition. Why should a person act out such audacity? A story tells how Rabbi Menahem Mendel of Kotzk was discussing the purpose of human existence with another

---

[99] Idem., *Tales of the Hasidim: Early Masters* (New York: Schocken, 1947), 105--7; see the previous story on the "strong thief" that precedes this , 104--5.

disciple of Rabbi Bunam.[100] When that disciple expressed the view that humans were meant to perfect their souls, Menahem Mendel objected. "That was not what our teacher told us. Humans were created to uplift the heavens." This view of the human purpose assumes that the world as it now exists is not perfect, that humans have the task of improving it, and that by improving it humans enhance godliness in the world.

Heschel recognized this aspect of Jewish teaching. He characterized the goal of Jewish mystics as seeking "the elevation and expansion of existence."[101] Humans have a role in making a chaotic world holier, of being partners with the divine in sanctifying reality. Such a view assumes a negative assessment of creation. The world remains in need of human assistance; it requires people to perfect it. Heschel affirms this aspect of creation. He notes that "If the Creator is at all concerned with His creation," then human beings with all their potential for both constructive and destructive actions must have a special part in the divine plan.[102] A negative view of creation suggests that human beings not only influence and shape the creation but also affect the creator. They interact on both the material level of this world and on the higher level of the spiritual world. God's

---

[100] Buber, *Later Masters,* 264.

[101] Abraham Joshua Heschel, "The Mystical Element in Judaism," in *The Jews* II. Louis Finkelstein, ed. (Philadelphia: Jewish Publication Society of America, 1949), 603.

[102] Heschel, *God in Search,* 171.

concern for the world manifests itself in a concern for humanity with humans playing a crucial role in improving the world.

The view that God has a concern for human action reinforces an impulse to human achievement. Heschel remarks that not only are humans partners with the divine, God participates and aids human endeavors. To remember this partnership provides people with assurance that they do not labor alone.[103] While human beings must remember that their actions are inadequate, they also need to recognize their need to act in extraordinary ways.

The term God may suggest aspects of the world serving as resources for human deeds. Understanding God as a partner with human actions suggests a world that is unpredictable and often disorderly yet also filled with unexpected supports for humanity and its efforts. Human beings often experience the world as poorly made and irrational. A logically consistent world, one directed by an intelligent creative force, would exhibit less wastefulness, duplication, and—from a human standpoint—fewer failures. The view of God as frustrated artist, as a wise inventor who nonetheless cannot succeed in carrying out the divine plan alone, corresponds to a common reaction when people face meaningless tragedy, wanton destruction, and incomprehensible stupidity. Environmental disasters, genetic disorders, scientific puzzles suggest that God's creativity lies outside of human understanding, logic, or moral rationality.

---

[103] Heschel, *Man is Not Alone*, 269.

Human beings inhabit a chaotic world that challenges them to make sense out of it. While normative teachings suggest living with the dilemmas of life, the charismatic teachings advise wrestling with what is unsatisfactory and seeking to improve and change it. This view may be disturbing, but it is a human reality. David Kraemer notes that the schools of Shammai and Hillel debated whether it would have been better for humanity to never have been created (see Babylonian Talmud Eruvin 13b) and that the conclusion was that while it would have been better never to have been created, since creation took place, a person must fulfill the divine will. Kraemer suggests "Not only does the conclusion as stated negate the essential goodness of human existence, it impeaches the wisdom of the God who created us."[104]

This disturbing view of the creator, however, does not impinge on or reduce human responsibility. In fact, using God as a symbol of the experimental aspect of nature helps reinforce human ambition to change reality. Whether the world fits with our mortal ideas of perfection and wisdom appears to be irrelevant. Humanity's duty toward the divine remains in force even if the world seems chaotic and unpredictable. People today may use the idea of a deity to encourage not only gratitude but also fortitude, a willingness to accept the challenge of making a less than perfect reality better and to remain steadfast in the face of inevitable disappointments, changes, and uncertainties.

In this way, humans must combine an acknowledgment of limitations set by the boundaries originally established by the

---

[104] David Kraemer, *Reading the Rabbis: The Talmud as Literature* (New York: Oxford University Press, 1966), 69.

divine with an audacity that propels them to creativity of their own. This combined personality depends on fulfilling more than the normal regulations of life. It requires an intention and attitude that transcends the ordinary and makes each person a charismatic hero advancing beyond the boundaries of the everyday to reach a new level of concentration and purpose.

That new goal represents a dynamic view of selfhood. The human self does not remain stagnant. Now it may exhibit virtues of humility; then it may exhibit virtues of ambition. In both cases new prohibitions and new injunctions flow from those virtues. In both cases the symbol "God" plays a useful role—either as a reminder of human ignorance or as an assurance that no person acts alone. Charismatic spirituality depends on such a foundation of a complex and variegated personality symbolized by an equally dynamic picture of the divine.

CHAPTER THREE:

Abraham Heschel, Charismatic Spirituality and The Nightmare of History

Abraham Heschel on the Nexus of History and Spirituality

Abraham Heschel saw an awareness of history as an essential element in developing religious spirituality.[105] Reflecting on the renewal of Jewish life in the Land of Israel, he contended that it anticipates the inner connection between mystery and history. The story of the Jewish people shows how historical events emerge from a spiritual relationship with the divine. History takes shape not as a random sequence of events, but rather as either an acceptance of a divine commission or a rejection of it. Most importantly, from his standpoint, spiritual history determines the meaning of human actions. Acknowledging the intertwining of history and mystery provides the underpinning of ethical awareness.[106] Becoming aware of how

---

[105] Susannah Heschel correctly notes that while critics sometimes date her father's interest in Zionism to 1967 and others suggest a tension between Zionism and her father's view of holiness in time, he never disparaged holiness in space or the importance of particularistic history. See Susannah Heschel, "Introduction," in Abraham Joshua Heschel, *Moral Grandeur and Spiritual Audacity: Essays Edited by Susannah Heschel* (New York: Farrar, Straus, and Giroux, 1996), xxv.

[106] Abraham Joshua Heschel, *Israel: An Echo of Eternity* (New York: Farrar, Straus and Giroux 1967), 97, 30, 118.

we shape history also brings awareness of human duties and obligations in creating history.

This perspective shows, first, that for Heschel history reveals whether or not human beings have fulfilled their true obligations. An awareness of history, therefore, stimulates charismatic spirituality because it raises consciousness of the demands and prohibitions placed on human beings. That connection between spiritual disciplines and historical insight needs further exploration as does the general shape of history as such. Heschel also insists on a teleological element in historical understanding—history begins with creation and moves to redemption. The *beginning* of history lies in the fact of a world, of human existence within reality. The *meaning* of history depends on its goal or purpose, on its final achievement. Thus Heschel claims, "The world is contingent on creation, and the worth of history depends on redemption."[107] How does an awareness that events stand in need of an ultimate purpose lead to a commitment to duty? How does a sense of historical destiny create a commitment to obligations and interdicts?

Heschel remarks that Jewish history is determined by "covenant," and that this history depends upon "faithfulness to the covenant."[108] The irony of this statement is that the covenant itself is part of "history." History as recalled, is, therefore,

---

[107] Idem., *God In Search of Man: A Philosophy of Judaism* (New York: Farrar, Straus, and Cudahy, 1955), 418.

[108] Ibid., 68, 216.

determinative of "history" understood as a general category. In this sense, Heschel correctly contends that "to believe is to remember."[109] History does not just dwell in the past; it dwells in those who remember it in the present. Covenant creates community through a common memory of the past, through a common commitment to the ends for which humanity strives, through an affirmation of the continued relevance of people and actions that have gone before. The term "covenant" refers less to an actual agreement made in the past than to attitudes in the present that evoke the past.

Heschel's thinking about history and spirituality, therefore, requires four investigations. First, the connection between spirituality and history needs amplification. Secondly, the general shape of history needs to be sketched and analyzed. The teleological element in the creation and evaluation of historical events needs identification and explanation. Finally, the continued presence of the past in contemporary living needs fuller exposition and description. Heschel couches his discussions in terms of Jewish theology. Nevertheless his depth-theology insists that the idea of a divinity concerned with humanity that "mysteriously impinges upon history" is common to all religions.[110] Exploring the implications of his ideas, even his particularistic emphasis on events such as the Nazi Holocaust and the renewed State of Israel, shows that Jewish teachings, despite

---

[109] Ibid., 213.

[110] Abraham Joshua Heschel, "From Mission to Dialogue," *Conservative Judaism* 21:3 (Spring 1967), 2.

their particularity, teach general lessons for a common human spirituality.

History and Spirituality

How are history and spirituality related? Spirituality does not arise in a vacuum. Spiritual experience is rooted in a particular time and place. Spirituality grows and develops within a specific historical context. Mircea Eliade writes that "Even the most personal and transcendent mystical experiences are affected by the age in which they occur."[111] Some thinkers, however, assert that spirituality transcends its historical context. They see it as a way of "opting out of the fight to be a man of power."[112] From that perspective history and spirituality stand opposed to one another. Spirituality points beyond the material history, beyond the tragedies and triumphs of life.

Jewish thinking often rejects such a division. Its spirituality emphasizes going beyond clear-cut dichotomies. The Russian philosopher Vladimir Soloviev celebrated the emphasis on corporality of Jewish theology. He recognized that Jewish spirituality stands at the crossroads between history and transcendence.[113] This chapter explores that spirituality and the

---

[111] See Mircea Eliade, *Patterns in Comparative Religion*. Rosemary Sheed, tr. (New York: Sheed and Ward, 1958), 2.

[112] Phillip Rieff, *Charisma: The Gift of Grace and How It Has Been Taken Away from Us* (New York: Pantheon Books, 2007), 21.

[113] D. Stremooukhoff, *Vladimir Soloviev and His Messianic Work,* Elizabeth Meyendorff, tr., Phillip Guilbeau and Heather Elise MacGregor, eds. (Belmont, MA: Nordland, 1980) and Jonathan Sutton, *The Religious Philosophy of Vladimir Solovyov: Towards a Reassessment* (New York: Macmillan, 1988).

76

way in which history, through sympathy with divine compassion for the suffering of the world, becomes the seedbed from which religious sensitivity creates a new set of commandments and prohibitions. Without an awareness of history and its meaning, without compassion arising from that awareness, charismatic spirituality cannot grow or flourish.

Responding to the reality of history may stimulate virtues that permit charismatic spirituality. Studying history places a person between the past and the future, and by doing this leads people to question their present. History provides a perspective on a person's responsibility. New duties and obligations may emerge from an immersion in historical memory. Sensitized to human needs and the inadequacies of life, people who take history seriously may create new patterns of behavior to cope with their sensitivity. One obligation placed on those seeking spirituality is that of an attention to historical realities.

Abraham Joshua Heschel, the Holocaust, the State of Israel, and History

Abraham Joshua Heschel faced two great historical realities of his lifetime—the Nazi slaughter of six million Jews (the Holocaust) and the rebuilding of a Jewish homeland in Israel. Both influenced his spiritual message. Hillel Goldberg divides Heschel's development into two parts. Before the Holocaust, Goldberg suggests, Heschel studied and wrote to reconcile his own conflicted soul. After the Holocaust he wrote and studied to heal the soul of every person.[114] That event had taught Heschel the meaning of history and its implication for a life of spirituality—a sensitivity to human suffering. The meaning of history ceased being a purely Jewish concern and became a property of depth-theology.

Heschel's fundamental assertion denies that history consists of disconnected, discrete events. History, he insists, follows a pattern—the pattern of covenantal responsibility. What occurs in history consists either of human obedience or disobedience to the divine will.[115] When human beings follow the God's plan, history shows positive attributes. When human beings disobey that plan, tragedy results. God suffers through history because human beings create tragedies. As John C. Merkle points out in his analysis of "the pathos of God" in Heschel, God participates in history because the divine responds to what human beings do.[116] God answers with compassion when humanity cries out in pain. Heschel sees the Holocaust as an indication that all history testifies to suffering and sorrow. He remarks that because of it even the moments of highest pleasure and satisfaction are tinged with sadness.[117]

---

[114] See Hillel Goldberg, *Between Berlin and Slobodka: Jewish Transition Figures From Eastern Europe* (Hoboken, NJ: KTAV, 1989), 128.

[115] Heschel, *God In Search of Man*, 68.

[116] See John C. Merkle, "Heschel's Theology of Divine Pathos," in his *Abraham Joshua Heschel: Exploring His Life and Thought* (New York: Macmillan, 1985), 72.

[117] Heschel, *Echo of Eternity*, 21.

78

The Holocaust, therefore, symbolizes more than just an event in Jewish experience. It does not stand as a unique event in history; it illustrates a general principle—that human actions bring tragedy to the world. The world itself changes because of the outcry against such tragedy. Political transformations are possible because reality responds to the sorrow wrung from suffering hearts. The agents for these changes and transformations are human beings sensitive to such cries and aware of the need to respond to them.

Heschel's view of Jewish political renewal in Israel, while guarded, remained within the framework of his understanding of history. In general he insisted that Jewish revival demanded a change of persons, not a change of political organizations. He denied that the purpose of Judaism was the survival of the Jewish people but rather the communication of spiritual ideas to all people.[118] Nevertheless, he hailed the new Jewish state as a harbinger of hope for all humanity. It represents God's response to suffering, showing how individual lives shaped by compassion create a better world. He considers it a symbol that human beings, not just Jews, may still hold out an expectation for a better life. He considers it a "promise" and a "recalling," but not a completed entity.[119] That completion awaits the end of history, but its hope animates all human endeavors and activity.

---

[118] Abraham Joshua Heschel, *The Insecurity of Freedom: Essays on Human Existence* (New York: Farrar Straus and Giroux, 1966), 226.

[119] Heschel, *Echo of Eternity*, 30--31.

Heschel contended that this message of hopeful criticism derives from a generally human response to tragedy—that of compassion. Although Jewish tradition links redemption to a specific political event, that of the Messiah and an ushering in of Jewish independence, Heschel finds in Israel restored hope for a universal redemption, a redemption for all humanity.[120] He calls Jerusalem a "seat of mercy" for all people.

Wherever human beings sigh, he imagines that Jerusalem responds with compassion. The activity of rebuilding Zion seems to him a symbol that hardship and suffering lead not just to a compassionate feeling but to actions arising from that feeling.[121] In this type of compassion Heschel saw the promise of a better humanity. The world today, he commented, has "an abundance of weapons but a scarcity of compassion." Only compassion, he thought, could rescue modern men and women from the trap of a world of violence. It is through acts of compassion that human beings find dignity and their sense of purpose. From such compassion they discover their duties to one another and to improving the world.[122] Compassion arises from an acknowledgement of history's nightmare, from a recognition of a previously existing human obligation.

Heschel's response to the particular history of modern Jews provides a guide not just for Jews but for all modern women and

---

[120] Ibid., 225.

[121] Ibid., 37.

[122] Heschel, *Insecurity*, 59, 180.

men who need to look to history to discover both its terrors and its promise. From a study of history people can cultivate compassion for others, a compassion born of recognition of the horrors being perpetrated and of the possibilities for spirituality. Heschel understood that while the Holocaust and the rebirth of a Jewish homeland were experienced by Jews they taught lessons for all people.

History, and Compassion

Heschel's intuition finds more general confirmation. James Joyce has Stephen Dedalus famously try to awaken from the nightmare of history, an effort that commentators see just as important for his later co-protagonist in *Ulysses*, Leopold Bloom, the Jew, as for the Irishman.[123] Heschel agreed with the first part of Dedalus' statement. He claimed that the prophets of the Hebrew Bible had already recognized that history is a nightmare.[124] He saw that, however, as a sign that humans have a responsibility to transform that nightmare, to improve the world, to refashion history in the image of God. Heschel compared the case of the prophets to that of Abraham who saw the world as a house in flames and realized that there must be someone who cared about what happened to it.[125] Disaster awakens sympathy for those undergoing it.

---

[123] See Neil R. Davison, *James Joyce, Ulysses, and the Construction of Jewish Identity: Culture, Biography, and "The Jew" in Modernist Europe* (Cambridge: Cambridge University Press, 1996), 235.

[124] Abraham Joshua Heschel, *The Prophets* (Philadelphia: Jewish Publication Society, 1962). 184.

God's suffering runs as a consistent theme through Jewish stories. God suffers when the Egyptians drown in the Sea of Reeds during the Exodus as well as when Israel undergoes exile and tribulation. When angels seek to rejoice at the destruction of Israel's enemies, God reproaches them. Divine compassion leads to divine awareness that the world requires a transformation. That compassion, however, takes shape through the actions and reactions of human beings. Indeed, while many stories suggest that great rabbis and early leaders petition God to end human troubles, one myth tells that God reprimands heaven, earth, the angels, the early leaders, and the great rabbis for not imploring for redemption. They are condemned for not taking God's suffering seriously enough to seek its end.[126] Humanity has an obligation to sympathize with others.

Heschel merges compassion for the victims of history with compassion for the author of history. Jewish spirituality emphasizes an all-embracing compassion extending to both creatures and the Creator. The spirituality that extends beyond therapeutic self-centeredness depends on recognizing the common human plight. Compassion entails more than just a feeling—it requires actions that address the suffering and distress engendering that feeling.

---

[125] See the discussion on this passage given by Heschel in his books *God In Search of Man*, 112--3, 267; and *A Passion For Truth* (New York: Farrar, Straus and Giroux, 1973), 272--3.

[126] See Howard Schwartz, *Tree of Souls: The Mythology of Judaism*. (New York: Oxford University Press, 2004), 519.

An interesting parallel to this theme occurs in stories about the Messiah, the central figure in the Jewish hope for world redemption and the focus of a later section here. In one such tale the Messiah agrees to accept his suffering only after recognizing the comparable pain undergone by the deity. Because of this God and the Messiah enter into a covenant anticipating the redemption of the world.[127] God requires that human beings, like the Messiah, recognize this situation; they have to develop compassion for the compassionate divinity who feels the pain and suffering of the creation.

The ethical principle of compassion toward everything in the world arises from an empathy with the creator of the world.[128] Jewish spirituality includes sensitivity to divine suffering as a precondition to an awareness of universal pain. The telling of Jewish history seeks to evoke sensitivity, compassion, and a means of communicating the common human condition and its hope for redemption. It demands a type of compassion that extends to transforming the world as a whole and not just Jewish life.

Compassion, Politics, and History

The Hebrew Bible understood that the relationship between disruptions that mark history and the ideal political structure

---

[127] Ibid., 483--4.

[128] See Peter Ochs, "Compassionate Postmodernism: An Introduction to Rabbinic Semiotics." *Soundings* 76, 1 (Spring 1993): 139--52.

require actions to overcome that discrepancy. Its authors created stories or myths to cope with those disruptions. Jewish thinker, and biblical scholar Martin Buber embraces the Bible's historicization of mythic tales. He contrasts "history" to "apocalypticism." The prophetic faith, Buber feels, emphasized history because within it human beings learned their responsibility. Not monotheism, he averred, but ethics lies at the heart of the Bible's revolutionary view. History takes on importance because human deeds change the world; people supply an element of surprise, of spontaneity to creation. Buber characterizes this prophetic insight that legitimates history as "the highest strength and fruitfulness of the Eastern spirit" because it declares that only a creature freely choosing its own deeds is "suited to be God's partner in the dialogue of history." He sees the choice between history and apocalypticism challenging every human society.[129]

Buber considers those societies which choose history "in league with the prophets."[130] While Buber does not use Heschel's phrase about the "nightmare" of history, he does see the messianic ideal of the kingdom of God as an act of compassion in

---

[129] Leo Strauss notes how Buber rejected Heidegger's view of the prophets as secure in "the certainty of salvation." He suggests that this rejection overlooks the messianic promise. Such was not the case, but for Buber that promise depends on human historical action. See Strauss' "Preface to Spinoza's Critique of Religion," in his *Liberalism: Ancient and Modern* (Ithaca, New York: Cornell University Press, 1989), 234--5.

[130] Martin Buber, "Prophecy, Apocalyptic, and the Historical Hour," in *Pointing the Way*. Translated and edited by Maurice S. Friedman (New York: Harper and Row, 1957), 192--207.

history, as evidence of Jewish spirituality working through and against the sweep of human events. He understands the prophets as exemplars of a charismatic spirituality that requires an acknowledgement of history and its problems as the precondition of its ethical demands.

Nahum Glatzer, presenting several of Buber's studies on the Hebrew Bible, declares that "The central theme in Buber's biblical research concerns the concept of the kingdom of God, the origin of the institution of kingship in ancient Israel, and the inception of the idea of the messianic kingdom."[131] The vision of the messianic age inspires compassion through history and transcends any particularistic historical narrative. While history itself is important, the messianic hope that transcends that history gives it meaning, purpose, and redemption.

Buber finds echoes of this vision in unlikely places. The Psalms, for example, contain an ancient myth calling for both a social and personal interpretation. This myth, occurring in several biblical texts and also in ancient Near Eastern writings, concerns the fall of a great national hero or even a leader who is identified with a divine being. The notion that every nation has a divine protector and that these angelic national representatives contend with one another characterizes many ancient Near Eastern theologies.

---

[131] Nahum Glatzer, "Editor's Postscript," *On Judaism*. Nahum N. Glatzer, ed. (New York: Schocken, 1967), 237.

This common belief becomes the basis for the drama expressed in Psalm 82.[132] That psalm has a clear theological point–Yahweh is the leader of the gods, the head of the divine council. Yet it also has a political point–Yahweh decides who are the true leaders and how they should function. The theological distinctiveness of the psalm, however, contrasts with the mythic representation of Yahweh as head of the divine council. That depiction has neither linguistic nor historical elements to mark it off from similar tales told either in the Hebrew Bible or in other ancient texts. The mythic substratum of the psalm is generic rather than specifically Israelite.[133] All societies require a compassionate understanding of history and a consequent ethical demand upon their leaders.

The psalm begins by announcing God's presence in the angelic court and continues with God's accusation that these gods are unjust. The psalmist then recognizes that the pagan deities are of no importance and will eventually be deposed from their high positions. Most scholars point to Isaiah 14:12-15 and Ezekiel 28:1-10 as examples of what may happen to such beings.[134] These passages have clear political objectives. They place Israel's national objectives within the context of international

---

[132] See Nahum N. Sarna, *Songs of the Heart: An Introduction to the Book of Psalms* (New York: Schocken, 1993) , 169--74.

[133] See Harry P. Nasuti, *Tradition History and the Psalms of Asaph*. SBL Dissertation Series 88 (Atlanta, GA: Scholars Press, 1988), 111.

[134] See John L. McKenzie, "Mythological Allusions in Ezekiel 28." JBL 75 (1956): 322--7.

struggles. The nation of Israel will triumph because the supernal representatives of such nations as Tyre, Egypt, or Babylonia have proven unworthy of divine favor. While mythic elements are used in these passages the prophetic writers make the political implication of the narrative central.[135]

The psalm moves beyond the telling of a myth to advocate its political message as a universal one. It ends with an invocation: the psalmist urges God to do in reality what the psalm projects him having done in the supernal realm. He, the just deity, should take the reins of government from the hands of the unjust gods. The mythical image remains in place: the heavenly council abides and controls sublunar life. Nevertheless the author hopes that God's own action will end the injustice of such a condition. A messianic vision redeems the world from the nightmare of history with a compassionate redemption for all.

Buber's treatment of the psalm shows how an imagistic evocation of the deity may recall and awaken the possibility of an I-You meeting, a type of charismatic spirituality responsive to the needs of the other with whom one interacts.[136] Buber's

---

[135] See Norman Habel, "Ezekiel 28 and the Fall of the First Man." *Concordia Theological Monthly* 28:8 (1967), 516--24.

[136] Martin Buber, *Good and Evil: Two Interpretations----Right and Wrong, Images of Good and Evil* (New York: Scribner's, 1953), 20--30 and his *Darkho Shel Miqra*, [Hebrew] (Jerusalem: Bialik Institute, 1964), 162. For a scholarly treatment of the psalm see Mitchell Dahood, *Psalms II, 51--100: Introduction, Translation, and Notes.* Anchor Bible (Garden City, New York: Doubleday, 1968), 268--71.

commentary characterizes the psalm as a polemic against understanding "the history of the human race as a continuation of the history of nature" and against "the delusion that the way of man can be determined from the general customs of the animals."[137] The members of God's council err because they engage in power politics. They assume that strength determines who deserves the governance of human life. Such a view makes charismatic spirituality impossible. Only leaders and a social order responsive to the nightmare of history can create the new pattern of interdicts and commandments associated with charismatic spirituality, a spirituality for which the psalm calls.

The psalm, on this reading, addresses the historical human condition, not some "cosmic circle of a heavenly host." The author of the psalm agrees that God does delegate authority and that heavenly princes may well adjudicate the fate of nations. Nevertheless, the heavenly principle of government, like the earthly one, remains the desire for justice.[138] The psalm teaches earthly rulers--who, like supernal ones, act as intermediaries between the divine being and the human community--that only justice legitimates their power. A true spiritual leader follows the dictates or compassion rather than the passion for control.

Buber traces the psalm back to a human experience, claiming that it only begins with the testimony of the psalmist a human being. Later, Buber suggests, the author translated his testimony about his life, into a literary work. That poem sought to

---

[137] Buber, *Good and Evil*, 28.
[138] Ibid., 25--27.

convey a vision that confirmed God as ruler over the world. Out of a private I-You meeting, the poet crafted a moral lesson: "those who were entrusted with the office of judge succumbed to injustice" but were themselves punished. The author moved from direct experience to a general lesson: the chaos of history does not represent the final truth. Ultimately righteousness, justice, and human concern for the afflicted prevail. This "true" experience of history counteracts "false" myths that evoke the pessimistic determinism.[139] Buber's analysis of the psalm places the idea of the Messiah within the context of compassion, spirituality, and the meaning of history.

Compassion for the suffering imposed by unjust leaders demands rectification of civil abuse. Buber's interpretation of Psalm 82 places a responsibility not only on leaders but on all who see how corrupt leadership undermines human existence. False leaders require opposition not for political expediency, but to ameliorate the suffering that they impose. Compassion leads people to take upon themselves political activism. Unless misguided leaders are replaced by morally responsible ones, countless tragedies will occur.

One way that charismatic spirituality arises from historical awareness is through sensitivity to injustice, through recognition that attaining justice may sometimes require moving beyond a present political order and creating a new one. Religious women and men, perhaps women even more than men, perceive how society creates inequality, causes suffering from systemic

---

[139] Ibid., 29--30.

injustice. From this perception they glean a compassion for that condition and then resolve to alter it. One inspiration for charismatic spirituality arises from that resolve. The resolve grows out of a renewed comprehension of the disruptions that bring unjustified suffering and pain to human beings. Awareness of history brings with it a recognition that the social order needs reconstruction, not by the application of some new criteria of justice but by a renewal of already existing standards.

Messianism, History and Obligations to Those Who Suffer

Not only political corruption but also the accidents of birth and social setting often lead to human suffering. The messianic intrusion on history illuminates such suffering. Heschel points to the long tradition of Jewish longing for redemption achieved only through a perfected humanity. He sees the renewal of Jewish life in Jerusalem as part of that tradition as cultivating God's dream for an ideal world, a messianic world.[140] Like the prophets, Heschel uses messianism, and in particular the messianic hopefulness of a restored Israel, to criticize the status quo.[141] That ideal takes shape as God responds to the imperfections of life. When human compassion cries out against the problems history poses, God answers through human beings who improve reality.

Messianism has taken many shapes in Jewish life.[142] Even rabbinic literature records debates about expectations of the

---

[140] Ibid., 48, 51,

[141] Heschel, *God In Search of Man*, 208.

Messiah. Modernists often took the messianic as a symbolic rendering of one or another theory of progress. Liberals interpreted the Messiah as a mythic symbol that humanity was becoming more and more rational. Marxists saw the dynamic of history unfolding in a predetermined patterned that owed as much to Jewish messianism as to Hegel.

For Hermann Cohen and other Kantians the traditional view of a personal Messiah was a mythic expression inherited from a primitive past. Hoping for some royal figure to transform the world was seen as a picturesque way of imagining a world in which the moral will is fully realized.[143] The idea of the Messiah, Cohen argues, rejects complaisant thinking. The Messiah represents human suffering and human activism. The messianic time will occur through continual progress, growth, and change, not through a process of eternal rebirth. Cohen concludes that for Jews judgment and divine justice are of the highest concern. True being does not come on its own; it must be earned by human

---

[142] See, for example, Harris Lenowitz, *The Jewish Messiahs: From the Galilee to Crown Heights* (New York: Oxford University Press, 1998) and the essays in Mark Cohen and Peter Schafer, eds., *Toward the Millennium: Messianic Expectations From the Bible to Waco* (Leiden: Brill, 1998). The material that follows makes use of my essay "Franz Rosenzweig and the Development of Postmodern Jewish Ethics," *Rosenzweig Yearbook 3* (Freiburg: Verlag Karl Alber, 2008) 71--97.

[143] Steven S. Schwarzschild, "The Democratic Socialism of Hermann Cohen," *HUCA* 27 (1956), 436--7.

struggle and striving.[144] The messianic ideal springs from and depends upon human compassion put into action.

One of the oldest messianic stories gives evidence of this view (Babylonian Talmud Sanhedrin 98a). Rabbi Joshua ben Levi who, according to legend, often met up with the prophet Elijah, once asked the prophet when the Messiah would come. Elijah told him to ask the Messiah himself and instructed him to go to the city of Rome. At the city gates he will see a gathering of beggars who are destitute and plagued by sickness. One beggar, unlike the others, will change his bandages one at a time rather than all at once. This is the Messiah who wishes to be ready immediately when God calls upon him and so does not want to delay by putting on several bandages.

Rabbi Joshua follows this instruction and does indeed meet the Messiah who answers him that he will come "hayom"— today. When Rabbi Joshua sees Elijah again he complains that the Messiah lied to him. Elijah explains that the Messiah was citing Psalm 95:7 "Today, if you would heed my voice." The Messiah suffers in the exile, but people by heeding God's call for compassion can redeem themselves and the Messiah.[145]

---

[144] See the discussion in Hermann Cohen, *The Religion of Reason: Out of the Sources of Judaism*. Simon Kaplan, tr. (New York: Frederick Unger, 1971), 244--91.

[145] This tale is reported by Howard Schwartz, *Tree of Souls: The Mythology of Judaism*. (New York: Oxford University Press, 2004), 492. He tells the story of the unsuccessful Messiah Joseph Della Reina next, 492--5.

Traditional Jewish teachings emphasize the need to bring the Messiah by using official means—obedience to the divine commandments. Nevertheless, spiritual leaders often allowed their compassion for the suffering of the Jews to inspire an activist program that went beyond this restriction. An entire genre of stories developed showing how misguided compassion for the Jewish people led certain spiritual leaders to act prematurely and thus bring disaster both on the Jews and themselves.[146] The purpose of these stories is ostensibly to warn against messianic claimants. Nevertheless the tales invariably suggest, at least in their original forms, the good intentions of the failed Messiah involved.[147] In the tales of such failed claimants people learn compassion for human struggle and the almost inevitable collapse of even the best of intents.

The development of the story of Joseph Della Reina shows the general structure. Originally the tale emphasized the sympathetic nature of Della Reina's hopes to bring the Messiah. Following the Kabbalistic teachings of Isaac Luria he engaged in magical attempts to hasten the final days. He addressed several supernal figures, including Elijah the prophet. Every time he

---

[146] See Eli Yassif, *The Hebrew Folktale: History, Genre, Meaning*. Forward by Dan Ben Amos. Jacqueline S. Teitelbaum, tr. (Bloomington: Indiana University Press, 1999), 311--12.

[147] See the tales of David Al--Roi and Joseph Della Reina in Pinhas Sadeh, *Jewish Folktales Selected and Retold by Pinhas Sadeh*. Hillel Halkin, tr. (New York: Doubleday, 1989), 237--8 and 246--7 and Micah Joseph Bin Gorion, *Mimekor Yisrael: Classical Jewish Folktales*. Emanuel bin Gorion, ed. I.M.Lask, tr. (Bloomington: Indiana University Press, 1976), 353--8; Bin Gorion also brings stories of other failed Messiahs 358--77.

demanded to know how to bring the Messiah and defeat Satan he was warned of the dangers and almost inevitable failure that he faced. Finally, he spoke with the angelic intermediary Metatron and discovered how to bind and capture that power of evil—Samael and Lilith. After doing this he followed the instructions given him for finding and binding these demonic figures. He managed to bring them under his power. Although he thought he was following the prohibition of giving them neither food nor drink, he did, however, allow them to sniff some snuff when they complained of faintness. That act was understood as offering incense to the demons, and he fell into their clutches. He went from one sin to another until he lost the power of repentance itself. In the end he committed suicide to save the Jewish people from the evils he had visited upon them. Nevertheless, he had honestly hoped to hasten the coming of redemption despite his ultimate failure.

Additional versions of the story added that he eventually converted from Judaism and even fell into the depths of black magic and the seduction of demons.[148] In the subsequent additions to the story the original emphasis on compassion becomes more and more diluted in order to provide a stronger warning against allowing such compassion to lead to actions that inevitably lead to greater problems for the Jewish people. The frequency of such tales, however, suggests that Jews continued to pursue the messianic vision despite continued warnings.

---

[148] See the versions in ibid., 837--52, the comments of Schwartz, *Tree of Souls*, 492--5, and the version given in Sadeh, *Jewish Folktales*, 237--8.

Compassion inevitably leads to action, even if action sometimes has unintended consequences. Heschel notes that Jewish thought insists upon messianic hope precisely because it recognizes the limitations of human actions and, while encouraging them, does not rely upon them:

> Indeed, messianism implies that any course of living, even the supreme human efforts, must fail in redeeming the world. It implies that history for all its relevance is not sufficient to itself.[149]

This statement makes three important points. The first is that human endeavors are doomed to failure. Messianic striving cannot, by itself, lead to redemption. Secondly, this fact suggests that history has meaning only as a reminder of human inadequacy. An awareness of history breeds an awareness of failure, of suffering, of the "nightmare." Finally, however, Heschel does not, thereby, reject either history or human struggles. Precisely because messianic efforts fail, humans must continue to hope and persevere in their actions.

The lessons here are ambivalent, but valuable. The first is that judging history by a messianic standard reveals the suffering that individuals undergo. That the Messiah suffers symbolizes the inadequacies and inequalities of society. Whether one believes in a literal Messiah who will come at the end of time or whether one believes in a messianic era of ideal human existence, the idea of a Messiah suggests that human existence here and now lacks equality and the tools necessary to create a fulfilled human life.

---

[149] Heschel, *God in Search of Man*, 379.

Religious people do more than seek to alter social structures. They take on the obligations of alleviating the suffering of individuals, of binding the wounds of the Messiah, that is of working to correct the conditions creating individual suffering.

Historical Figures and a Common Memory

Heschel not only located hope in the critical notion of the Messiah. He also sought to uncover the mystery hidden in what appear to be "natural" events. Ordinary events only seem to be insignificant; they conceal the extraordinary.[150] These events take on significance as memory links them to the past. Heschel insists that religious thinking draws on two sources—personal insight and memory.[151] Memories of the past—both historical and personal—illuminate how every moment presents an opportunity for spiritual living. Remembering religious heroes of the past enables people in the present to recognize the divine demand, the call to compassion for others, in the situations they face.[152] He celebrated Jerusalem as a place that reminded people never to be "immune from the intrusion of the past's moments."[153]

Jewish communal identity depends on just this sense of the past as a present reality. Figures in Jewish history often stand as spiritual heroes worthy of emulation in the present. The patriarch

---

[150] Heschel, *Echo of Eternity*, 51.

[151] Heschel, *God In Search of Man*, 27.

[152] Ibid., 140.

[153] Heschel, *Echo of Eternity*, 30.

Abraham not only symbolizes obedience to the divine and compassion to all creatures but intrudes into history to affirm these values. Heschel remarks that someone who affirms the covenant with Abraham, continues the life of Abraham.[154] Heschel realized that community takes shape as people recognize the demands made upon them in the present as a continuation of a task set ages before them. He defined Jewish identity as a cooperative existence—"living in the Jews of the past and with the Jews of the present."[155] A look at how Jews express that conviction shows that compassion arises from such an understanding of history's relevance in the present.

Stories tell how Abraham not only initiated the ceremony of circumcision but in every age actually appears when a quorum of Jews is needed to perform it.[156] He appears in a similar fashion to support a pious cantor, to provide an answer to a Muslim vizier, or to remind a rabbi of the need to welcome the poor into his Sukkah on the holiday.[157] Similar tales involve Elijah the Prophet who returns to earth periodically to remind people of the need for compassion and to reward those who are compassionate. Even King David intrudes on later history in this fashion. Perhaps most strikingly in these stories is one in which a rich man shames

---

[154] Heschel, *God in Search of Man*, 201; see also his *Man's Quest for God: Studies in Prayer and Symbolism* (New York: Charles Scribner's sons, 1954), 88.

[155] Heschel, *Man's Quest*, 45.

[156] See Sadeh, *Jewish Folktales*, 36.

[157] Ibid., 35--38.

a poor reciter of psalms and escapes punishment only when the Baal Shem Tov reminds David of his own failings.[158] Spiritual heroes of the past reappear in the present to teach Jews the necessity of compassion and the duties springing from it.

One unique tale draws upon the figure of Jonah the prophet.[159] According to the story the hero's father told him never to take an oath, even if that to which he swore was the truth. Unscrupulous people took advantage of the man because of this. In desperation, he fled his own country, but disaster upon disaster occurred—his wife and two sons seemed to drown either in the ocean or in a river. In despair, he sought to end his life. Nevertheless, the prophet Jonah appeared to him and counseled him not to give up hope. Following the advice given him by Jonah the man eventually regained everything that he had lost.

The point here goes beyond Jonah. Indeed, this same story is retold in many different sources with different figures serving to save the desperate man[160] The point is that spiritual heroes exercise compassion throughout history and not only during their own historical period. Awareness of this continuing charismatic spirituality reminds people of the expectations and obligations they must fulfill, of duties that have been incumbent on them throughout past history.

---

[158] Ibid., 45--7.

[159] Ibid., 154--8.

[160] Ibid., 430.

The story about Jonah's rescue of the desperate man illustrates how a common past surfaces in the present to give authenticity and power to a general idea, the idea that compassion surpasses the vagaries of ordinary life. The community that shares this history does so in order to evoke compassion, understanding, and a sense of continuity in which the virtues of the past reappear in the present. The values considered important by the community are, by mentioning the heroes of the past, located in a historical context and not merely in the lived present. These tales show how reliance on the past can lead to a supportive community and to unexpected success. More often, however, stories have tragic rather than happy endings. A different sort of community arises from that understanding of history and the duties flowing from it.

Jews together with all who seek to strengthen and build community can learn from this view of history. Memory of how heroes in the past ministered to human suffering and intrusion of that memory into present existence reinforces common bonds linking people together. Compassion for the victims of history leads to a spiritual grounding dedicated to answering the needs of the individual.

God's role in the nexus between spirituality and history is that of inspiring a recognition of both the nightmare and promise of events. Heschel comments that God's revelation occurs "not primarily in the facts of nature. ... He spoke through the events of history." God's voice in history provides an understanding of divinity derived from human response rather than as a personification of some external force. The term "God" refers first to the sense of outrage sensitive people feel when history's nightmare becomes a scandal and requires human protest. It may entail other, more anthropomorphic, secondary meanings. Nevertheless, reference to the deity stands primarily as a way of reminding people of their own often dormant feelings that challenge injustice and suffering.

Ascribing to God the judgment that history requires amelioration means that compassion arises from a source beyond ordinary perception. Using the language of spirituality turns the gap between historical reality and the ideal world into a problem rather than a fact of nature. This gap inspires the compassion that breeds spirituality by crossing barriers of time to view the present from the perspective of eternity. New interdicts arise—those forbidding the causing of suffering—and new injunctions—those inspiring an improvement of the world. The use of covenant language serves a similar, although distinctive, purpose. That language suggests a continuity through time and among human beings with common concerns. Remembering historical precedents inspires a communal identity uniting people in the struggle to act compassionately.

While the stories within the Jewish tradition illustrate such a communal identity, they also point beyond the particularistic example. All people share in the grand history of humanity. All people suffer from the nightmare of history and hope for a better world. Examples of compassion unite such spiritual figures as the Buddha, Kwan Yin, Saint Francis, and Mother Theresa.

CHAPTER FOUR:

Heschel, Culture, Spirituality and Generosity

Abraham Joshua Heschel, Culture, and Pluralism

Abraham Joshua Heschel recognized the necessity for religious pluralism in the modern world. He called that diversity "the providence of God," and noted that "God is greater than religion."[161] Religion represents social and cultural constructions created by humanity in response to the divine call. God stands for the universal demands people feel impelling them to justice and righteousness. Religion and the voice of God interact so that as people respond to divine demands, the social structures change. He insisted that individuals interacted with their political and social environment; society influences them, but they are also builders of that society. Because individuals help shape the social environment, social ills are symptomatic of personal failures. The "public climate of opinion," he argued influenced the spirituality of each person and individual crime "discloses society's corruption."[162] This interplay of the individual and the social grows out of the necessity each person has of sharing in and contributing to culture.

---

[161] Abraham Joshua Heschel, *The Insecurity of Freedom: Essays on Human Existence* (New York: Farrar Straus and Giroux, 1966), 181.

[162] Ibid., 93.

The idea of culture is often debated and contested.[163] In the context of this present study it refers to the artistic, literary, and behavioral expressions of a particular human group. Culture, Heschel thought, grew out of spirituality. It represents the inner life of a person projected outward toward others. Culture, he claims, is itself a product of human spirituality. Human beings create culture as they project their inwardness outward. Unless individuals discover their unique spiritual and personal identities, no society can exist. A vital and vibrant social order depends on individuals who have allowed their inner natures to express a transcendence and higher unity.[164] Culture, in this sense, is the opposite of crime. It represents the triumph of concern for others over concern for the self; it expresses a moral sensitivity that reaches beyond personal gain born of heeding divine commands.[165] It expresses social responsibility not selfishness.

That sensitivity to social obligations expresses itself in a pluralism that generally reaches out to others, sharing insights and gleaning insights as well. Heschel suggests that we all have become "a single neighborhood" in which religious isolation is a

---

[163] See for example the opening section of Leo Strauss, "What is Liberal Education," in his *Liberalism: Ancient and Modern* (Ithaca, New York: Cornell University Press, 1989), 3--4.

[164] Abraham Joshua Heschel, *Man is Not Alone: A Philosophy of Religion* (New York: Farrar, Straus and Giroux, 1951), 180.

[165] Abraham Joshua Heschel, *God In Search of Man: A Philosophy of Judaism* (New York: Farrar. Straus, and Cudahy, 1955), 171.

"myth," a dangerous falsehood that threatens spirituality.[166] Such a situation calls for new ways of interaction, for new opportunities for communication between people. Modernity demands a spirituality that calls forth cooperation and sharing. The virtue of generosity becomes an essential aspect of charismatic spiritual living in contemporary life. Such generosity grows in the soil of human culture once that term is clearly understood.

The Significance of Culture and Spirituality Among Jews

Charismatic spirituality depends on a particular attitude toward culture, no less than toward personality and history. Discussing the meaning of cultures begins by distinguishing between what Immanuel Kant called "culture" and what he called "civilization."[167] Culture refers to those human expressions that arise from humanity's confrontation with nature. Cultural productions represent how people interact with their environment to make it more conducive to human life. These expressions humanize a hostile world and give it an order, a beauty, and sense of meaning. They enhance human freedom and therefore point to

---

[166] Abraham Joshua Heschel, "From Mission to Dialogue," *Conservative Judaism* 21:3 (Spring 1967), 2--3.

[167] See the discussion by Natan Rotenstreich "Enlightenment: Between Mendelssohn and Kant," *Studies in Jewish Religious and Intellectual History*. Siegfried Stein, and Raphael Loewe, eds. Presented to Alexander Altmann on the Occasion of His Seventieth Birthday University, (Alabama: The University of Alabama Press, 1979), 263--76.

what "a rational being produces out of his own choice" and therefore reinforce the morality of human decision-making.[168]

Civilization, by contrast, imposes an external order, a socially obligatory code, a sense of proper decorum. Charismatic spirituality and the restrictions of civilizations will be the subject of the next chapter. Here, however, the focus is on culture and cultural creations. The natural generosity implicit in human creativity expresses itself in culture and finds a receptive audience from those who have not lost that generosity themselves. Cultural exchange reveals the generous human soul. Jewish history exemplifies this interchange.

Efraim Shmueli has pointed to seven distinct "Jewish cultures."[169] He interprets Jewish history as a contest in which differing leadership groups strive to establish their system of meanings and symbols as dominant. He notes several tensions within that struggle—between universalism and nationalism, the individual and society, religion and the state, reliance on the past and orientation to the future.[170] What Shmueli contributes to a

---

[168] Ibid., 277. Accepting this definition and distinction between culture and civilization makes Nietzsche's criticism of culture as "the reduction of the beast of prey man to a tame and civilized animal" (Friedrich Nietzsche, *Basic Writings of Nietzsche*. Translated, edited, and with Commentaries by Walter Kaufmann [New York: Modern Library, 1992], 478) a reference not to "culture" but to "civilization."

[169] See Efraim Shmueli, *Seven Jewish Cultures: A Reinterpretation of Jewish History and Thought*. Gila Shmueli, tr. (Cambridge: Cambridge University Press, 1990).

[170] Ibid., 112--39.

theory of Jewish culture is the recognition of both the diversity of its content such that there is no single culture of the Jews and also the continuity of the dynamics by which any such culture develops. The variety of Jewish cultures arises from the contact between Jews and non-Jews. That contact provides a resource for Jewish spirituality. The inner conflict among Jews reflects differing cultural influences on distinctive Jewish communities and their views of reality.

Jewish cultures influence spirituality by introducing new demands and expectations derived from contact with non-Jewish others. Culture in the context of this chapter points to several discrete elements having a "family resemblance" to each other.[171] In this case there are three points of resemblance—the cultural products are produced by individuals or groups self-identified as "Jews," whatever meaning they ascribe to that term, these works claim to contribute to a definition of that term or to express an aspect of it, and, finally, these creations address the relationship among people calling themselves "Jews" to one another and to those whom they consider "non-Jews." Jewish culture as described here, then, represents a Judaism conscious of and often oriented toward a world filled with "others" who are not part of their community. That response to others suggests a widening of concerns often associated with increased spirituality.

This association of culture, spirituality, and a broadened social outlook suggests what many understand as the critique of

---

[171] See the review article by Yuval Jobani, "Three Basic Models of Secular Jewish Culture," *Israel Studies* 13:1 (2008): 160--9.

the therapeutic interpretation of modernity.[172] While some argue that an increased focus on individual spiritual development leads to a type of narcissism, others dispute that claim. They find that generosity expresses a trust in the world, a concern for others, and willingness to beyond traditional limits. This last is extremely important. If spirituality includes what some refer to as "nontradition-centered religious beliefs and practices," it necessarily trespasses boundaries. Nonetheless, it may also inspire a greater sense of responsibility, of new obligations, and of increased recognition of duties to those outside of the tradition.[173] Findings correlate the exploration of innovative ways of expressing religiousness with an equally expansive approach to other aspects of life, an inherent generosity found in both an approach to religion and to the others among whom one lives.[174] An exploration of Jewish cultures shows how charismatic spirituality inspires an integrative and expansive approach to non-Jews, both as bearers of cultural gifts and as partners in the ethical task of improving the world and enhancing human life generally. That example underlies Heschel's recognition of the new expectations placed on spirituality in the modern world. Modern culture grows out of a renewed understanding of

---

[172] See Michele Dillon, Paul Wink, Kristen Fay, "Is Spirituality Detrimental to Generativity?," *Journal for the Scientific Study of Religion*, 42:3 (Sep., 2003): 427--42

[173] Ibid., 432.

[174] Ibid., 439.

pluralism and expresses a spirituality sensitivity to diversity and the cultivation of variety within any human society.

Jewish Cultures and Their Formation

From its very beginnings Jewish cultural expression has used forms and material from non-Jewish sources. Scholarly consensus agrees that the narrative and legal sections of the Hebrew Bible draw freely on and were influenced by those of other ancient Near Eastern traditions.[175] Later Jewish creativity also draws upon and utilizes elements from external groups and communities. A double dynamic ensues—Jews borrow from and adapt the cultural expression of the environment in which they live and they also contribute to that environment enriching it. Generosity drives this dynamic—a generosity of the environment toward Jews and of Jews toward the environment.

Rabbinic literature shows evidence of this dynamic. Alexander Altmann analyzed what he thought of as "a strange view of creation."[176] According to this doctrine God wrapped himself in a tallit (a fringed prayer garment) and light issued forth to create the world. As Altmann notes this view of creation reflects a neo-platonic perspective. He also shows that dialogues

---

[175] See Joseph Blenkinsopp, *The Pentateuch: An Introduction to the First five Books of the Bible.* The Anchor Reference Library (New York: Doubleday, 1992), 194--204; Simon B. Parker, *Stories in Scripture and Inscriptions: Comparative Studies on Narratives in Northwest Semitic Inscriptions and the Hebrew Bible* (New York: Oxford University Press, 1997).

[176] See Alexander Altmann, "A Note on the Rabbinic Doctrine of Creation," in his *Studies in Religious Philosophy and Mysticism* (Ithaca: Cornell University Press, 1975), 128--39.

among rabbinic masters and between such masters and Hellenistic figures make it clear that this view should be kept secret, minimized, or at least surrounded by mystery. Later Jewish thinkers debated this view as well, with the medieval thinker Moses Maimonides confounded by it and mystical thinkers critical of Maimonides for his reluctance to accept it.

These debates and vacillations show an energetic interchange among Jews and between Jews and non-Jews in their intellectual cultural expressions. That interchange reflects a concern for spiritual truth beyond the confines of a single tradition. It recognizes that Jews and non-Jews may learn from one another and derive spiritual and religious inspiration from each other.

Gerson Cohen, focusing on what he calls "the variety of rabbinic cultures" postulates three general ways in which Jews have interacted with the cultures of Western civilization (again, the concept of "civilization" in a slightly different context and with a different definition is the subject of the following chapter).[177] First, Jews have passed on the idea of an "eternal" scriptures that remains valid even as it is reinterpreted at different times and in different places. This legacy not only infuses Jewish life with a warmth and sensitivity but also allows new ideas and forms to emerge and be integrated with traditional texts. This concept allows Jews to accept non-Jewish generosity and

---

[177] See Gerson D. Cohen, *Studies in the Variety of Rabbinic Cultures* (Philadelphia: Jewish Publication Society, 1991).

generously invites non-Jews to view their own texts in a similar way.[178]

Secondly, Jews have responded to antagonism with both a readiness for martyrdom and a commitment to the details of their traditional cultural expressions. In this way they have shown that loyalty to a self-definitional set of activities expresses human dignity in the face of hostility. They justify retention of certain identifying cultural marks as a commitment to the divine.[179] Society requires the diversity created by independent groups living according to their distinctive creativity.

This intransigent devotion to identity often takes the form of a political protest. Cohen considers the Jewish commitment to the idea of the Land of Israel and its eventual messianic rebuilding as a critique of all human political forms. This form of political skepticism finds expression not only in Jewish ideology but also in many other, so-called secular, protests against a political status quo.[180] Such a criticism suggests the value of a variety of cultural expressions rather than a single culture. While discontent with society forms the focus of the next chapter, here that discontent is important for its expression of the positive importance of diversity.

---

[178] Ibid., 63--68.

[179] Ibid., 80--84.

[180] Ibid., 87--89.

Whether or not Cohen is correct in his assessment of rabbinic contributions to general culture, his thinking does suggest the interactive play of influences that occurs even when the cultural environment within which Jews live is hostile. This dynamic continues in later thought as well. While many thinkers attribute the rise of Jewish historiography in the sixteenth century to the impact of the expulsion from Spain, others contend that this trend imitates the general approach of humanism and Renaissance thinking in general.[181] Jews shape their self-understanding in response to the categories and intellectual structures of the thought around them.

The example of such a pluralistic sense of culture suggests the type of open generosity demanded by charismatic spirituality. While the examples that follow look at Jewish cultural interaction with non-Jews, they serve more generally as illustrations of the ways one culture shares with another. No single culture remains aloof and distant from the subcultures in its midst. Spirituality may grow out of personal experience; it develops, however, only through its exchange with others, an exchange that can take different forms and express itself in various ways. If the term "God" refers to the ground on which culture flourishes, then cultural pluralism indeed represents the divine will.

---

[181] See Mordechai Breuer, "Modernism in Sixteenth--Century Jewish Historiography: A Study of David Gans' Zemach David," *Jewish Thought in the Sixteenth Century*. Bernard Dov Cooperman, ed.(Cambridge: Harvard University Press, 1983), 49--88.

Jewish Cultures in Hellenistic Times

One of the most challenging examples of Jewish culture and its diversity occurred during Hellenistic times. Some Jews created a cultural life in contrast to the ideas and attitudes of the Greco-Roman world. Others accepted part of the Hellenistic tradition, but rejected other parts. Still other Jews refashioned Jewish life in accordance with the ideals associated with Greek thought and expression. Studying the differing Jewish groups in Hellenistic times, Albert I. Baumgarten sees the basis for self-differentiation in such things as food, dress, marriage, commerce and worship. He suggests that this sense of difference in ancient times parallels the rise of sectarianism in contemporary life.[182] These elements represent the self-expression of a group, a pattern of behavior that distinguish members of one society from those of another, tokens by which people display their affiliation to one or another social association. While diversity separates groups, it can also enrich each group with new perspectives.

The Hellenistic world, as Salo Baron remarks, required such self-conscious social markings since its worldview had "torn down many barriers separating peoples from one another" and developed a common ideology that pervaded the Western world.[183] Even the most identifiably Jewish of rabbinic writings, the *Mishnah*, reflects Greek thought and philosophy. As Jacob

---

[182] See Albert I. Baumgarten, *The Flourishing of Jewish Sects in the Maccabean Era: An Interpretation*. (Leiden: Brill, 1997), 7, 199.

[183] Salo Wittmayer Baron, *A Social and Religious History of the Jews* Volume I: Ancient Times, Part I (New York: Columbia University Press, 1952), 173.

Neusner points out, its organization and structure follows the logic of the Hellenistic thinkers of its time.[184] This Hellenistic condition in which Jews both draw upon the cultural environment in which they live and devise new cultural expressions of self-differentiation stands, paradigmatically, as the model of Jewish culture generally.

The significance of Jewish culture, as indicated by its Hellenistic development, lies in its relationship to non-Jewish culture. To create Jewish culture meant to navigate the waters of a non-Jewish world.[185] Jews may justify this accommodation to others on the basis of a messianic expectation. Eventually such cultural acceptance will give way to purely Judaic forms of expression. Nevertheless, as a realistic and normative pattern such borrowing from and allowance for non-Jewish culture remains a necessity. Jews share a common experience with non-Jewish others; they envision a solitary and exclusive world of their own. They mediate between the two through mechanisms that allow a flow of influence in two directions. Those

---

[184] See Jacob Neusner, "The Greco--Roman Philosophy of Judaism: The Mishna in Context," *Bits of Honey: Essays for Samson H. Levey.* Eds. Stanley F. Chyet and David H. Ellenson (Atlanta, GA: Scholars Press; 1993), 63--92. (South Florida Studies in the History of Judaism; v. 74). Compare his *Judaism as Philosophy: The Method and Message of the Mishnah* (Columbia, SC: University of South Carolina Press, 1991).

[185] See Steven D. Fraade, "Navigating the Anomalous: Non--Jews at the Intersection of Early Rabbinic Law and Narrative," *The Other in Jewish Thought and History: Constructions of Jewish Culture and Identity.* Laurence J. Silberstein and Robert L. Cohen, eds. (New York: New York University Press, 1994), 145--65.

mechanisms not only represent the basis for Jewish cultures but also the foundation of an ethical concern—that of generosity. This generosity assumes that Jews will always live among and interact with a community of non-Jewish others. Without the sense of this generosity Jewish spirituality during their exile in the nations would have been impoverished. Some of their most characteristic expressions grew out of an exchange with their environment.

The generosity indicated here is that of cultural humility. While different groups do indeed create specific cultural artifacts, those should never be assumed an isolated or unique set of creations. Cultural arrogance, no less than individual arrogance, undercuts spiritual life. Any group that asserts its superiority or even exclusivity has misunderstood its own history and creativity. Human spirituality never exists in a vacuum. Only a generosity of spirit that admits the debt any culture owes to outsiders represents itself honestly. The general lesson taught by the experience of Hellenistic Jews is that even the most distinctive products of a group must be acknowledged as the result of interaction with others and must result in a sharing with those outside the group.

Diaspora and Culture

The history of Jewish spiritual creativity attests to the reality of cultural sharing. A fascinating variety of Jewish tales reinforce the idea that many Jews prefer staying in the lands of their dispersion, living in what is technically "exile" from their homeland, than in returning to the Palestinian environment from which they came.[186] Extraordinary evidence comes from the Hellenistic period in Alexandria, Egypt. The story, preserved in the Apocrypha but found elsewhere as well, tells how the Septuagint translation of the Bible came into being.[187] The Emperor Ptolemy sought to gather all the great books of the world into a single library. On discovering that the Jews had a compendium of wisdom in their sacred scriptures, he ordered them translated. That translation occurred through several miraculous events. Because of this translation, Jews were honored and secure in Hellenistic Egypt. This story reveals Jewish willingness to share their teachings with others and that of others to turn to the Jews to enrich their own lives.

The same idea echoes through a famous story that also takes several forms—that of a boy stolen from his home after he has merely learned to read the first book of the Bible, Genesis (*Bereshit*).[188] The tale tells how this lad ends up in a foreign kingdom the ruler of which is suffering from a spiritual crisis. He has discovered a book in a language he cannot fathom, actually it is the Bible. The lad recites it and translates it for the king who finds in its wisdom a cure for his worries. Whether the story shows its Hellenistic roots by calling the king Caesar or merely speaks of some anonymous "ruler," the point remains the same.

---

[186] See Micah Joseph Bin Gorion, *Mimekor Yisrael: Classical Jewish Folktales* III. Emanuel bin Gorion, ed. I. M. Lask, tr. (Bloomington: Indiana University Press, 1976), 348--51.

[187] See Ibid., 249--52.

[188] Ibid., 601--3.

When Jews go to a foreign country they bring the gift of their teachings with them.

This paradigm derives, at least in part, from the biblical story of Joseph (Genesis 37-47) in which the hero is stolen from his homeland, enriches the land to which he comes, and eventually brings his entire family to that place. A key idea in this story, however, emphasizes a "sojourn" in the foreign country. The time spent in Egypt is an "exile" from which the family will eventually be liberated and return in triumph to the homeland. For many Jews, however, that exile has become merely a dispersion, a scattering into distant places without the hope or desire for a return. For these Jews the boundaries between "natives" and "foreigners" has become blurred in a common sense of a new identity in a new social setting. That new identity brings with it the possibilities of new obligations and expectations, of a new charismatic spirituality. The new responsibilities of these Jews create a new cultural reality. The biblical pattern repeats itself again and again so that what appears "new" actually recapitulates a cycle from before. The "new" culture reflects a type of positive symbiosis for which all modern women and men need reminding again and again.

Nowhere is this view more prevalent than among Jews in the United States of America. Unlike European Jews, Zionism for American Jews never implied a negation of the Diaspora, a rejection of their new home in favor of a return to their original home. American Jewish thinkers from colonial times through the present, whether Zionist or non-Zionist, have sought to understand their lives in the Diaspora and their relationship to the

Land of Israel as an ideal, to the condition of Jews throughout the world, and, since the late nineteenth century, to the idea of an independent Jewish State, expressing their views in often controversial and emotional ways precisely because they affirmed the Diaspora as a positive factor in Jewish existence.

Much of the writing concerning views of the Diaspora focuses on American Zionism and its distinctiveness from conventional Zionism.[189] Almost unanimously, American Jews "reject the Israeli notions of exile" and find the traditional Zionist view of Diaspora life as "precarious, distorted, and incomplete" unacceptable.[190] Far from embracing a "therapeutic" return to the comfort of an independent, self-contained Jewish culture, American Jews celebrate the specific duties and responsibilities arising from being a member of more than one cultural tradition. More recently the idea of Diaspora or Exile has been advanced as a central motif in human self-understanding and post-modern theories of identity.[191] This recognition of the universal value of

---

[189] This section draws on my essay "Great American Jewish Thinkers and their Attitude towards Diaspora," *Encyclopedia of the Jewish Diaspora: Origins, Experiences, and Culture*. Volume 2: Countries, Regions, and Communities. M. Avrum Ehrlich, ed. (Santa Barbara, California: ABC--CLIO, 2009), 566--70. See Naomi Wiener Cohen, *American Jews and the Zionist Idea* (New York: Ktav, 1975); Steven M. Cohen and Charles S. Liebman, *Two Worlds of Judaism: The Israel and American Experiences* (New Haven: Yale University Press, 1990); Melvin I. Ursofsky, *American Zionism From Herzl to the Holocaust* (Garden City: Doubleday, 1975).

[190] Cohen and Liebman, *Two Worlds,* 93.

[191] See the discussion in Benedict Anderson, *Imagined Communities: Reflections on the Origin and Spread of Nationalism* (New York: Verso New Left Books, 1983), and David Biale, "The Melting Pot and Beyond: Jews and the Politics of

living in more than one culture typifies the thought of American Jews.

The pattern of looking at Diaspora life positively runs throughout American Jewish history. From the earliest Jewish leaders in the New World through contemporary American Jewish thinkers, life in the Diaspora generally, and in the American Diaspora in particular, has been affirmed as an integral part of Jewish existence. During the Colonial period through the American Civil War the general view espoused considered Diaspora Judaism a valid replacement for the ancient Israel-centered faith as American Jewish leaders became impatient with the "Palestinian messengers" in America.[192] American Jews hailed America as a new Zion and their places of worship as a New Jerusalem. This trend has continued and, especially among Reform Jewish thinkers, has found recent proponents. While Zionists may condemn this view, it recapitulates an honored tradition within American Jewish life.

Later generations of Jewish thinkers, including Reform, Conservative, Orthodox, and Reconstructionist, have tempered this positive view of Diaspora with an acknowledgment of the importance of the Land of Israel and the historical memories of

---

American Identity," *Insider/Outsider: American Jews and Multiculturalism*. David Biale, Michael Galchinsky, and Susannah Heschel, eds. (University of California Press, 1998), 17--33.

[192] See Salo Wittmayer Baron, *Steeled by Adversity: Essays and Addresses on American Jewish Life* (Philadelphia: Jewish Publication Society of America, 1971), 158--266.

the Jewish people. American Jews became reluctant to reject Zionism after the creation of the State of Israel in 1948. Even so, an affirmation of Zionism was usually combined with a declaration of appreciation, loyalty, and validation for Jewish life outside of the Land of Israel and particularly for the Diaspora Jewish community within the United States of America.

This legitimation of the Diaspora took many forms. Some thinkers emphasized the creativity of Jews in the Diaspora; others saluted the international perspective and universalism cultivated by those living outside of Israel; still others considered landlessness a political benefit for the Jewish people. Finally, more recent thinkers have valorized a sense of exile and alienation cultivated by Diaspora living as an expression of an existential reality. All modern people can arguably be considered displaced persons living in "exile". Likewise, it has been argued that the Jew in Diaspora symbolizes the marginalization necessary for true moral perspectives. All these differences show that while American Jews affirm the Diaspora, they differ in their understanding of that affirmation. Rather than share a single culture, they have developed several distinct, if not competing, expressions of what it means to adopt, adapt, and transform Diaspora living. In this way American Jews institutionalize and universalize a cultural generosity without which charismatic spirituality could not flourish.

The generosity associated with living in Diaspora might seem restricted to Jews. In another sense, however, all people live in diasporas. We are all marginal to one or another cultural setting. We all move in and out of cultures, never being fully rooted in a single one. This sense of dynamic cultural movement suggests a permanent state of Diaspora existence, a homelessness even in the midst of a culture that we call our own. People respond to the restlessness this brings in different ways. Suspicion and hostility often mark interpersonal relationships because of the uneasiness one party feels. Yet a generosity of spirit can embrace the dynamism of contemporary life. Such generosity toward others and toward oneself allows for spiritual growth and development. Charismatic spirituality calls for an acceptance of homelessness by reminding people of the inherent generosity within any cultural community.

Cultural Understandings and Misunderstandings

While Jewish cultures draw from and seek to engage with the non-Jewish world around them, they sometimes misread the symbolic language of their environment. One familiar story takes the fact of Jewish-Christian debate and disputation and makes it the basis for a joke. Such disputations were, certainly, not usually funny or taken lightly. Jewish leaders found themselves forced to defend their beliefs, justify rabbinic documents such as the Talmud, and prove false the accusations of Jews who had converted to Christianity. To achieve this end, they needed to understand and be able to manipulate the cultural expressions of Christian intellectuals. Perhaps the most famous of the disputations was the one conducted in Barcelona with Rabbi

Moses ben Nahman. In each case, a common cultural legacy permitted this exchange.[193]

By contrast the humorous story that follows suggests a lack of cultural connection.[194] The tale recounts how an antisemitic priest reported to the king that Jews were disloyal since they expected one day to become a great and powerful nation. He demanded a debate with a Jewish representative which, if he won, would entail that the Jews could be banished from the land. The king agreed and summoned the Jews to select a champion. All the people lamented since none wished to face the priest and try to answer his questions. The town fool, however, volunteered to perform the task.

The priest stipulated that the dispute be carried out using signs rather than words. The fool agreed. The priest reached into his pocket and took out an egg; the fool took out some salt. The priest raised two fingers; the fool raised one. The priest took a handful of barley seeds and scattered them on the ground. The fool grabbed a hen to eat up the seeds. The priest turned to the

---

[193] See the various discussions in Jeremy Cohen, *The Friars and the Jews: The Evolution of Medieval Anti-Judaism* (Ithaca: Cornell University Press, 1982), Charles B. Chavel, *Ramban: His Life and Teachings* (New York: Philipp Feldheim, 1960), Robert Chazan, *Barcelona and Beyond: The Disputation of 1263 and Its Aftermath* (Berkeley: University of California Press, 1992), and Daniel Lasker, *Jewish Philosophical Polemics Against Christianity in the Middle Ages* (New York: Ktav, 1977); second edition (Portland, Or: Littman Library of Jewish Civilization, 2007).

[194] See Pinhas Sadeh, *Jewish Folktales Selected and Retold by Pinhas Sadeh*. Hillel Halkin, tr. (New York: Doubleday, 1989), 299--300.

king and admitted that he had been defeated. The Jew had responded correctly to all his challenges.

The king demanded an explanation since he could not follow what had taken place. The priest explained that he had used the egg to show that Jews are two-faced being different inside than they are outside while he interpreted the Jew's salt to signify that Jews are to the world what salt is to food. He had raised two fingers to imply that Jews serve both God and money; the Jew's single finger reaffirmed monotheism. The scattering of seeds alluded to the Jewish Diaspora, while the hen that ate them he thought referred to God's use of history to finally unify the Jewish people. The king was amazed by this explanation and by how the Jew had decoded the priest's symbols.

The Jewish populace, equally confused by what had happened crowded around the fool. The fool explained that he thought the priest would throw the egg at him, so he showed that he could throw salt in the priest's eyes. He interpreted the priest's two fingers as a gesture meant to poke out his eyes, so he had raised one finger to suggest that he could still ram it down the priest's throat. When the priest threw down the barley the fool felt it a waste and so let the hen to have some use out of it.

This story is meant as a joke, but it implies a type of cultural generosity. The different interpretations of the event show that the fool and the priest were using different symbols or cultural tools. Their points of reference were so different that they could easily misunderstand each other. Nevertheless, each generously attributed to the other a meaning derived from his own culture. A willingness to interact characterizes the life of the

Jew in the Diaspora. In this story that willingness has a positive conclusion, even if the event itself shows cultural confusion. The generosity necessary for charismatic spirituality overrode the differences of meaning between the two parties. When Jews and non-Jews shared a single culture, however, the debate could be serious and sometimes fatal. Nevertheless other stories suggest that a shared culture often has positive results—by understanding Christianity, Jews can improve their social status.

One story tells of the Spanish Jewish philosopher and biblical commentator, Abraham Ibn Ezra and his understanding of Christian culture.[195] All historical data suggest that Abraham Ibn Ezra lived as a Sephardic Jew, writing both Hebrew and Arabic, and being more at home with Muslims than Christians. The story, however, discounts this historical data. According to this tale Ibn Ezra had been taken captive and was up for sale as a slave (no historical evidence backs up this claim). A Christian bishop, recognizing the wisdom of the Jews, purchased this slave.

The king was seeking a viceroy and sent a message to the bishop. Although they had not met, the message said, the bishop could become the king's viceroy. If the bishop could answer three questions set by the king, then he could be appointed viceroy. If he failed to answer them, his life would be forfeit. The three questions were to indicate the direction God faces, the worth of the king, and what the king was thinking. The bishop was so disconcerted that Ibn Ezra noticed and asked him to

---

[195] Ibid., 220--1.

explain his problem, and when he heard it volunteered to go to the king in his stead.

Before facing the king, Ibn Ezra went to the market and purchased a silver crucifix for ten copper coins and a tallow candle. When he entered the king's presence, the ruler asked him first in which direction God faces. Ibn Ezra lit the candle and told the king that first he should tell him in which direction the candle gave out light. The king replied that it gave out light in every direction. Ibn Ezra replied that just so God faces in every direction. The king then demanded to know his worth. Ibn Ezra replied that it was nine coins. The king grew angry and asked him to explain himself. Ibn Ezra took out the crucifix. He told the king that he had just paid 10 coins for this. How could a mortal king be worth more than the image of the divine? He was powerful, but less so than God; therefore if the image of God is worth 10 coins, the king must be worth nine. The king accepted this answer, laughingly, but then demanded that Ibn Ezra tell him what he was thinking. The Jewish scholar replied, "You are thinking that I am the bishop, but in fact I am Abraham Ibn Ezra the Jew."

The king was delighted and sought to make Ibn Ezra his viceroy. Instead Ibn Ezra merely asked for his freedom which he received with gifts as well. The bishop became viceroy since his wisdom had brought about the meeting between Ibn Ezra and the king. Because Ibn Ezra could argue like a Christian, because he knew the cultural symbols that religion demanded and shared a similar view of the world, both he, as a Jew, and the bishop, as a

123

Christian, succeeded. Both held to the same valuations of secular and religious leadership and expressed those fearlessly.

The story shows how a shared culture, generously uniting Jews and Christians leads to prosperity and welfare for both. Ibn Ezra, defender of Jewish tradition has become a symbol of the importance of learning and understanding Christian ideas. In this way a historical figure apparently hostile to Christianity became a hero of charismatic spirituality illustrating the generosity of cultural sharing.[196]

Cultural generosity here combines with both personal and social awareness. Ibn Ezra clearly looks at his benefactor with gratitude. He takes a personal risk in going to the king on behalf of his patron, the bishop. The story also shows a generosity in learning and affirming the religious symbolism of the bishop. Ibn Ezra's victory would not have been possible had he not internalized the meaning and significance of Christian beliefs.

---

[196] Leo Strauss in his, ""On Abravanel's Philosophical Tendency and Political Teaching," in *Isaac Abravanel: Six Lectures*. J.B. Trend and H. Loewe, eds. (Cambridge: University Press, 1937), 93--129, argues that while Abravanel was influenced by Christian anti--monarchic views, other Jews were not. Abraham Ibn Ezra is noted as being singularly monarchic in his interpretation—perhaps as a reaction against Christian interpreters, 119. The use of Ibn Ezra in this tale, then, is extraordinary. Other tales do focus on Abravanel (Sadeh, *Jewish Folktales*, 222, tells how a courtier seeks to have Abravanel removed from royal favor and ends up suffering the fate he had hoped his rival would experience). Heschel himself used Abravanel as an example of what happens when Jews assimilate to the general culture. He suggested a benefit to the exile from Spain since it saved Jews from being a party to the excesses of the conquistadores—see Susannah Heschel, "Introduction," in *Abraham Joshua Heschel, Moral Grandeur and Spiritual Audacity: Essays Edited by Susannah Heschel* (New York: Farrar, Straus, and Giroux, 1996), xvi.

Ibn Ezra shows no hostility to Christian thought nor is his presentation to the king ironic.

The lesson taught by this story, in contrast to the tale of the town fool, is that cultural generosity implies taking seriously the beliefs of others. Respecting the differences of others means accepting the seriousness with which they take their faith. This type of cultural generosity applies to more than just Jews and Christians. Modern men and women need to do more than "tolerate" those with whom they disagree. They need to attribute the same depth of feeling and meaning to the beliefs of others as to their own beliefs. Only such a generous acceptance of the ideas of others can lead to that creative interaction upon which charismatic spirituality depends.

Generosity to Persons: Stories of Rashi

The figure of Rabbi Solomon ben Isaac, known by the acronym RASHI (1040-1105), looms as one of the most important leaders in Ashkenazic Jewish history. He organized the Jews of France and Germany into a cohesive system governed by rabbinic leadership. He built his institutions on the cultural expressions of his time including the pervasive use of French and the interchange between Jewish and non-Jewish clergy.[197] Legend

---

[197] See the following important studies: Maurice Liber, *Rashi*. Adele Szold, tr. (Philadelphia: Jewish Publication Society of America, 1906); Herman Hailprin, *Rashi and the Christian Scholars* (Pittsburg: University of Pittsburg Press, 1963); Salo W. Baron, "Rashi and the Community of Troyes." *Rashi Anniversary Volume* (New York: American Academy for Jewish Research, 1941), 47--71; Robert Chazan, *Medieval Jewry in Northern France: A Political and Social History* (Baltimore: Johns Hopkins University Press, 1973).

surrounds the story of his life, but one theme seems to predominate—that of generous intercultural sharing.

The sources provide conflicting accounts of both the date and place of Rashi's birth. One common myth states that his father possessed a precious jewel that he eventually threw into the sea.[198] Some accounts of this tale reflect hostility between Jews and non-Jews. Isaac, Rashi's father, in one account throws the jewel into the waters to escape Christians who seek to wrest it from him. In another tale Isaac's wife informs him that the jewel, if sold, will be used to decorate a bishop's vestment. Rather than have it serve a religious usage, Isaac disposed of it. The change of focus from the wife to the husband may reveal a not insignificant theme in Jewish storytelling.

Another version of the story, however, suggests that Isaac was about to sell it to adorn a heathen idol and, when his conscience bothered him, managed to appear to drop the jewel accidentally. This variety of narrative suggests that while some sense of hostility toward the Christian society existed, it often was repressed. The general point, however, emphasizes Jewish exclusiveness rather than inclusive generosity. The other, whether designating a bishop or a heathen worshiper, stands as a symbol opposed to and thus antagonistic to Jews.

Another tale provides evidence of that dual generosity marking Jewish cultural expressions. In this tale the meeting of human persons rather than symbols leads to a positive rather than

---

[198] See Liber, *Rashi*, 11--12 and compare Bin Gorion, *Mimekor Yisrael*, 759--60.

negative interaction.[199] Rashi, according to this story, travelled to the Orient. There he met up with a monk and began a theological dialogue. During their stay at a certain inn the monk became ill, and Rashi tended him. Later during Rashi's period as leading rabbi in France and Germany, he came to the dukedom of the Duke of Vratislav. There the Duke had him imprisoned and summoned before the Bishop of Olmutz. The bishop recognized Rashi as the Jewish scholar who had healed him when he was a monk and rescued him from the clutches of the duke. Here the negative element in the environment turns out to be the secular power. The Christian clergyman responds to Rashi's generosity with generosity of his own.

The difference between the story of Rashi's conception and of his meeting with the bishop is striking. When we encounter other people as human beings, generosity flows naturally. We see that they are suffering the same diseases, the same problems, and the same challenges as we ourselves. When we respond to others as fellow humans, we cannot help but minister to their sicknesses, alleviate their troubles, and assist them in their lives. The reciprocal generosity represented by Rashi and the bishop presents a model for all interactions between people who disagree with one another. When they see the other merely as a symbolic opponent, they tend toward hostility and distance themselves. When they see the other as part of an entire human community in which all are implicated, they act with generosity and kindness. That model suggests that in addition to a cultural generosity

---

[199] Liber, *Rashi*, 21--22.

arising from shared social constructions and ideas human beings can instigate a personal generosity by imagining a broader more universal culture.

Religious Equivalencies and Shared Culture

The key to creating such a culture of universality and generosity often lies in recognizing the common elements that all human beings share. Not everyone will agree to recognize those elements, but when they are accepted a culture may flourish. One illustrative story takes place in Baghdad after the Muslim culture began to flourish under the Abbasid rulers. Saadiah Al-Fayyumi (882-942) describes how a certain Abu Umar, a Muslim traditionalist visiting Baghdad from Spain had attended a philosophical meeting there. The first time he went he was scandalized to find not only sectarian Muslims but "unbelievers of all kinds." He was shocked that discussants were "limited to rational arguments." When he attended a second meeting the visitor remarked, "I found the same calamity there." He therefore resolved never to attend such a meeting again.[200] This shows the antagonism of an uncultured Muslim to the open culture shared by Muslims, Jews, and Christians alike. The cultural oasis that Baghdad had become would have been sterile without just that cross-fertilization to which Ibn Umar objected.

The beginning of the modern age of Jewish emancipation recapitulated the themes and shared culture of the era when

---

[200] Cited by Alexander Altmann in "Saadya Gaon Book of Doctrines and Beliefs," in *Three Jewish Philosophers* (Philadelphia: Jewish Publication Society of America, 1960), 13.

Baghdad flourished. Jews in Germany, in particular, cultivated the manners, values, and philosophical approach of their contemporaries. Moses Mendelssohn (1729-66) represents one of the foremost exemplars of a Jew sharing such a culture and seeking to enable other Jews to follow his example. He translated the Hebrew Bible into German in an effort to hasten the acquisition of the culture in which Jews lived. He also wished to use the translation to encourage Jews to enter the modern world and adapt to the general German culture.[201] For this adaptation to take place, the non-Jewish world needed to open itself to Jews. Only an emancipated Jewry could feel free enough and secure enough to engage in such a cultural unification. For most of his life Mendelssohn found an ally in the Christian thinker Gotthold Ephraim Lessing (1729-81).

Lessing wrote several dramas illustrating his faith in the Jews as rational, virtuous human beings. His most famous such play, *Nathan the Wise*, contains a notable scene retelling an old story meant to breed tolerance among differing religious groups and a fascinating picture of the divine.[202] This tale tells of a king with a magic ring that makes him beloved of all people. The king

---

[201] See Alexander Altmann, *Moses Mendelssohn; a Biographical Study*(University, AL: University of Alabama Press, 1973); Edward Breuer, *The Limits of Enlightenment: Jews, Germans, and the Eighteenth--Century Study of Scripture* (Cambridge: Harvard University Press; Harvard University Center for Jewish Studies, 1996); David Sorkin, *Moses Mendelssohn and the Religious Enlightenment* (Berkeley: University of California Press, 1996).

[202] See *Dramatic Works of G.E.Lessing*. Ernest Bell, tr. and ed. (London: William Clowes and Son, 1878), 305--9.

has three sons. When he dies he bequeaths an identical ring to each son. Which son has the true ring? Only his actions and the responses to them will tell which is the worthy son. That is the test of each of the three religions. Each religion must prove its validity by its deeds and none may actually possess the "true" ring.

The Jewish Sephardic tradition tells a similar tale.[203] In this story King Don Pedro II is urged to go to war against the Jews. The king summons a Jew who identifies himself as Ephraim Sanchez. The first half of his name indicates his Jewish character, the nature of the culture he has inherited and that he generously shares with Don Pedro. The second part of his name reflects his pride in Spanish culture and his acceptance of the generosity offered Jews by their non-Jewish neighbors. In himself this Jew mirrors the double generosity that represents the cultural virtue treasured by Jews. The king asks him whether he thinks Judaism superior to Christianity, to which the Jew replies that Judaism is better for him but Christianity is better for the king.

The king rejected this reply saying "I asked you about the beliefs themselves, not about their value relative to the believers." The Jew asked for three days to consider the question. When he returned he told the king that he had just received a problematic case to solve. A jeweler had gone on a journey and left two precious jewels behind—one for each of his two sons. The sons now demanded to know which jewel was better. He contended that only the jeweler himself could tell that. The king

---

[203] See Bin Gorion, *Mimekor Yisrael*, 444--6.

agreed with that answer, and so the Jew replied that the same held true for religions—only God can tell which if any of them is better and why. The king applauded the Jew's answer. Religions are equivalent to one another even while preserving their differences. Charismatic spirituality depends on recognizing this reality. An attempt to make one or another religion exclusive would reduce the rich diversity of human cultures.

This story shows the basis for the virtue of generosity to lie in a type of humility. Religions may claim absolute truth. That claim, however, has no external verification. While God appears in the anthropomorphic guise of father or king, the divine itself remains absent, beyond the appeal to authority. Direct testimony from God must be replaced by imagining the divine intent, determining God's emotional stake in the plurality of religions. Both believers and religious leaders need to recognize the limitations of their affirmations.

Heschel considered the "agony of history" to lie in the failure to respect other people's commitments; he argued that such respect is neither a political nor social norm but rather a religious insight.[204] This realization suggests that human beings can only make use of the treasures they have been given to make the world a better world. Jews and non-Jews cooperate in these efforts, each using the special tools given them.

God, understood from this perspective, stands for an emotional affirmation of the pluralistic impulse that motivates the creation of the most productive societies. The term stands for the

---

[204] Heschel, *Insecurity*, 181.

source of that necessity requiring generosity in accepting and sharing cultural expressions, in understanding and respecting the beliefs of others to such an extent that we can articulate them ourselves, and in perceiving the generally human community of which we are all a part. The generous interchange between all people ensures that gifts will be put to good uses rather than evil ones. More importantly, from their interaction new configurations of restrictions and injunctions emerge. Charismatic spirituality can create enhanced ways of shaping and channeling the interaction between diverse cultures.

CHAPTER FIVE:

Questioning Civilizations: Heschel, Spirituality and Caution

Abraham Joshua Heschel's Questioning of Civilization

Mordecai Kaplan has famously (or infamously) called Judaism a "civilization." His use of that term was inconsistent and reflected the changing currents of the time in which he wrote.[205] As if responding to this claim, Abraham Joshua Heschel announced that "civilization is not our religion." Indeed, he suggested Judaism in particular, but all religion generally, consists of the art of surpassing civilization.[206] Heschel's life exemplified this art. He consistently challenged assumptions and questioned established norms. Susannah Heschel, his daughter, correctly notes that theologically he was an iconoclast (another appropriate term would be "maverick") who, upon his death, was transformed into an icon.[207] He probed the problems of

---

[205] See Noam Pianko, "Reconstructing Judaism, Reconstructing America: The Sources and Functions of Mordecai Kaplan's 'Civilization'." *Jewish Social Studies,* New Series, 12:2 Mordecai Kaplan's "Judaism as a Civilization": The Legacy of an American Idea (Winter 2006): 39--55.

[206] Abraham Joshua Heschel, *The Insecurity of Freedom: Essays on Human Existence* (New York: Farrar, Straus, and Giroux, 1966), 233.

[207] Susannah Heschel, "My Father, Myself," *Bridges: A Jewish Feminist Journal* 14:1 (Spring 2009), 13. See the entire article, 1--11. Susannah Heschel identifies her own approach with that of her father—questioning the status quo and seeking new perspectives, 15. Compare her comments in Susannah Heschel, "Introduction," in Abraham Joshua Heschel, *Moral Grandeur and Spiritual Audacity: Essays Edited by Susannah Heschel* (New York: Farrar, Straus, and Giroux, 1996), xxviii

contemporary civilization and declared it on "trial" because of its depravity and lack of humility. Only a renewed spirit—one that he associated with the Jewish Sabbath—could lead people to surpass this civilization.[208]

His view of the Sabbath clearly emphasized Heschel's critique of civilization. He described the Sabbath drawing on the life and teachings of the mystical rabbi Shimon Bar Yochai. Rabbi Shimon, he explained, began by being outraged by the society in which he lived. Finally, he realized that not just that civilization but any civilization was problematic. For him: "All civilization, the worth of worldly living, became the problem."[209] An important aspect of depth-theology for Heschel is the recognition that civilized life poses more dilemmas than it solves. The appropriate religious response is not acceptance of civilization but rather a challenge to it, a questioning of its assumptions.

Several elements combine in Heschel's challenge to civilization. At times he seems to criticize the skeptical attitude typical of modernity. He declares that we have created a new "golden rule": suspect your neighbor as you suspect yourself.[210]

---

[208] Abraham Joshua Heschel, *God In Search of Man: A Philosophy of Judaism* (New York: Farrar, Straus, and Cudahy, 1955)), 418; compare the statements in *Insecurity*, 190, 218. On the association of the Sabbath with transcending civilization, see his *The Sabbath: Its Meaning for Modern Man*, Expanded Edition (New York: Harper and Row, 1966), 27.

[209] Heschel, *The Sabbath*, 37--38.

[210] Heschel, *Insecurity*, 17.

134

People must learn to trust their potential for doing significant actions.

Nevertheless, he applauds self-doubt. He wonders about leaders who think that they know what is right. He encourages political skepticism. He shudders at the thought of "people who are absolutely certain of their wisdom," and argues that the world needs a sense of embarrassment.[211] The framers of civilization require a challenge, they need a reminder of their fallibility; they must confront an iconoclast who questions their wisdom.

Heschel stood as that corrective figure necessary to keep political leaders humble, a figure essential for reminding people of the limitations of civilization. Traditionally, Jewish mysticism has played just such a role. Heschel notes that for the mystic the world in its outward form is not enough. The mystic plunges more deeply into life, holding together the seen and the unseen, the actual and the potential. In this way the mystic seeks to surpass the status quo and achieve what lies beyond the everyday. By its very nature Jewish mysticism questions civilization.[212]

While Heschel drew consciously on the mystical tradition, he also recognized the need to confront the political status quo on behalf of the oppressed and the unappreciated. His most famous

---

[211] Abraham Joshua Heschel, *Who is Man?* (Stanford, CA: Stanford University Press, 1965), 114.

[212] Throughout his essay on Jewish mysticism, Heschel makes its criticism of ordinary perception clear. See his "The Mystical Element in Judaism," in *The Jews* II. Louis Finkelstein, ed. (Philadelphia: Jewish Publication Society of America, 1949), 602--23.

stance was that on behalf of civil rights, but he also spoke up for the rights of patients, the poor, and the homeless. Susannah Heschel testifies that both she her father would take the arguments from the civil rights movement as a basis for feminism. She and her father, she avers, never disagreed about feminism, and he supported her efforts to assert women's prerogatives in Jewish practice.[213] Abraham Heschel criticized civilization both from the perspective of a mystic and a social critic; as a maverick he questioned the way civilization regarded the outcasts of society and also how it ignored the depths of meaning hidden behind the outward forms of daily life.

Heschel's stance as critic of civilization suggests an attitude important for the development of charismatic spirituality. That spirituality arises from a discontent with the ordinary framework of daily life. Some may think that advocating more freedom for those on the margin of society because of gender, sexual orientation, status, or economic standing represents a therapeutic liberation from normative restraints. In fact, as Heschel clearly understands, recognizing the oppression of these groups requires a greater sense of obligation, a deeper prohibition on harming others, and a new set of rules and interdicts that go far beyond those of conventional society. Citizens may hide from their responsibilities to others through the conventions designating one group or another as marginal to the social order. Those discontented with civilization challenge such citizens to activate a spirituality requiring more rigorous expectations. Civilization's

---

[213] Susannah Heschel, "My Father, Myself," 13, 15.

discontents remind citizens of what they have lost by becoming civilized and of the necessity to be skeptical of the claims civilization makes upon them. Those claims often conflict with the prior claims made by life itself.

Spirituality, Civilization and their Discontents

Theorists of modernity have realized that society produces discontents. Sigmund Freud, who has been called a moralist without a moral message, identified the tension produced by the conflicting coercions of nature and civilization.[214] He recognized the purposes of civilization and the reactions to it from individuals forced into such a constraining mold. He postulates that all civilization breeds its discontents. He may use the German word "kultur" but he implies the restrictions that restrain people from realizing their desires.[215] Human beings, he contends, seek an unattainable goal—that of happiness. They find this goal impossible for three reasons—the limitations of their own physical bodies, the exigencies of living in a hostile, and the requirements of living with other people. This latter imposition, he thinks, causes the greatest pain.[216] Humans, to exist in society, must necessarily thwart their own search for happiness.

---

[214] See the discussion throughout Philip Rieff, *Freud: The Mind of a Moralist.* Third Edition (Chicago: University of Chicago Press, 1979).

[215] Sigmund Freud, *Civilization and Its Discontents*. James Strachey, tr. and ed. (New York: W. W. Norton and Company, 1962), see especially 36ff. On the use of "civilization" to translate "Kultur" see the editor's introduction, 5--6.

[216] Ibid, 24.

While this view is apparently pessimistic, Phillip Rieff admits its validity.[217] He affirms its usefulness and understands it as a basis for spiritual development. Rieff comments that "Character is sacred order inscribed upon the body." Self-control over physical desires leads to personal growth. He claims that Freud recognized both this effect on individuals and on culture as a whole even though his "wild" disciples may have celebrated a "therapeutic" liberation from it.[218] Such a recognition means that while Freud identified sublimation as a fact of civilization, he also posited a morality requiring it. Freud knew that human beings need the restraint of civilization and that morality begins by embracing that restraint without the crutch of civilization's coercion.

People use various strategies to cope with the inevitable discontent produced by civilization. Among these, Freud implies, is that "oceanic feeling" some thinkers associate with "religion." Lost in such a dream of limitlessness and perfection people can transcend their inevitable pain and disappointments. He identifies civilization, therefore, with "spirituality" and warns of the tensions that spirituality brings.[219] Freud, therefore, suspects "religion." He sees it as an escape from the truth that civilization necessarily brings discontent in its wake.

---

[217] Rieff, *Mind of a Moralist*, 197.

[218] Ibid., 381.

[219] See the discussions of these ideas in Freud, *Civilization*, 60, 191, 266.

Like several other thinkers from ancient times onward, he assumed that religion inevitably plays a supportive role in civilization. Even if religion is an untrue narrative, it serves to stabilize social life.[220] These thinkers misunderstand the critical role religion often fulfills in challenging the social order. Both mystics and spiritually aware citizens generally often recognize the necessity of recalling the sacrifices civilization demands, sacrifices often unequally taken from the population. Frequently conventional conceptions of spirituality reflect the power of elite institutions. These conceptions require a new type of interpretation—one based on a skeptical approach, what has been called a hermeneutics of suspicion to liberate spirituality so excluded groups and individuals can discover it.[221]

Modern society requires a hermeneutics of suspicion as a foundation on which to develop new spirituality. From Freud onwards scholars have recognized the positive value of such an approach. Modern women and men require this type of skepticism animated their relationship to the constraints of living

---

[220] Leo Strauss seems to have found this type of argument in Lucretius. He suggests that for him "Religion thus appears to be a human invention which serves the purpose of counteracting the indifference of the whole to man's moral and political needs" even if he "wishes to remain silent about religion as a possibly pleasant and salutary delusion." See Leo Strauss, "Notes on *Lucretius*," in his *Liberalism; Ancient and Modern* (Ithaca, New York: Cornell University Press, 1989),100, 110.

[221] As will become clearer below, women's movements have recognized this reality most powerfully. See Shelley Finson, "Feminist Spirituality Within the Framework of Feminist Consciousness," *Studies in Religion/Sciences Religieuses* 16:1 (1987): 74.

with others.[222] Charismatic spirituality demands more of people than a mere affirmation of conventional injunctions and prohibitions. Only a spirituality that insists on new renunciations and obligations can overcome the stagnation of modern civilization. Only then they can move from the subconscious acceptance of civilization that creates discontent to a conscious morality with even greater discipline and restraint.

Women, Discontent, and a Virtue of Suspicion

From the Hebrew Bible onwards, Jewish women have symbolized the discontent arising from human disappointment with civilization. That discontent emphasizes the reality of choices, of differences, and of the necessity for diversity. Women seem to be in the forefront of such an ethics of suspicion of institutions. Robert Alter notes that there is a "remarkable gallery of women" who find the institutions of male authority immoral or lacking insight and compassion and who take the initiative in challenging them.[223] Women's subversion of an oppressive patriarch occurs frequently, as several feminist scholars have noted.[224] Awareness of this occurrence aids in the development of

---

[222] On Freud's hermeneutics of suspicion see Paul Ricoeur, *Freud and Philosophy: An Essay on Interpretation*. D. Savage, tr. (New Haven: Yale University Press, 1970). Ricoeur also emphasizes that this modern era has been characterized by suspicion.

[223] Robert Alter, *The Art of Biblical Narrative* (New York: Basic Books, 1981), 146.

[224] See the articles in Mieke Bal, ed. *Anti--covenant: Counter--Reading Women's Lives in the Hebrew Bible*. Bible and Literature Series, 22. (Sheffield: Sheffield Academic Press, 1989); Phyllis Trible, *Texts of Terror: Literary--Feminist*

a charismatic spirituality. Recognizing how patriarchy requires women to negotiate their spiritual life leads to a decision to alter the social order.

One typical example of such a situation occurs in I Samuel 1-2. The tale relates how the pious Elkanah has two wives— Penina and Hannah. While Penina has many children, Hannah has none. Elkanah tries to comfort Hannah by saying that he is worth more than children, but she refuses this rationale. She goes before the priest Eli who mistakes her heartfelt pleas as the ravings of a drunken woman. When reprimanded by Hannah, he gives her his blessing. Hannah dedicates the child who will be born to God's service. When the child is weaned and delivered to Eli, Hannah recites a psalm of praise—taking for herself the prerogative of a priest to utter such words. Eventually her son displaces the priesthood with a new power source, prophetic authority.

This story takes place in the context of the dissolution of the priestly hegemony of Eli and his family and the beginnings of new institutions in ancient Israel—prophetic critics and royal leadership.[225] Hannah represents a woman who goes beyond the status quo. Eli reveals his own weaknesses (he calls her a

---

Readings of Biblical Narratives. Overtures to Biblical Theology 13 (Philadelphia: Fortress, 1984).

[225] See the discussions in James Ackerman, "Who Can Stand before YHWH, This Holy God? A Reading of 1 Samuel 1--15." *Prooftexts* 11 (1991): 1--24; Marc Brettler, "The Composition of 1 Samuel 1--2," *JBL* 116 (1997): 601--12; Serge Frolov, *The Turn of the Cycle: 1 Samuel 1–8 in Synchronic and Diachronic Perspectives.* BZAW 342. (Berlin: de Gruyter, 2004).

worthless woman when, in fact, his own sons are the worthless ones). She may even be imitating Eve by asking for a son from God rather than from a human source (the redacting editor may have changed her request for a "child from the divine" to "a child from men.").[226] Hannah becomes a catalyst for that change which alters biblical institutions forever. She not only shows the weakness of present institutions but by her actions begins the process that will substitute new institutions for older ones. Her son Samuel will initiate the new order of prophets that replaces the priesthood represent by Eli. Not coincidentally one of the last of that new order is a woman, Hulda the Prophet, who provides the basis for a more developed social system under a constitutional leadership (2 Kings 22-23). The story of a woman brackets the prophetic system of the Bible.

The apocryphal story of Susannah and the Elders in the Daniel cycle shows a similar perspective.[227] Susannah in each of the versions we have received is an innocent victim accused by lascivious leaders of the community of sexual impropriety. The stories emphasize her status as someone who knows the law and

---

[226] See Michael Carasik, "Why Did Hannah Ask for the 'Seed of Men"? *JBL* 129:3 (2010): 433--6.

[227] See the discussion in Eli Yassif, *Hebrew Folktale: History, Genre, Meaning.* Jacqueline S. Teitelbaum, tr.; Forward Dan Ben Amos. (Bloomington: Indiana University Press, 1999), 61--63, although I disagree with his assessment that the folktale elements are associated with a female audience concerned about family purity. See the versions of the story presented by Micah Joseph Bin Gorion, *Mimekor Yisrael: Classical Jewish Folktales* III. Emanuel bin Gorion, ed.; I. M. Lask, tr. (Bloomington: Indiana University Press, 1976), 202--6.

has expertise in both legal and ritual process.[228] In the story in the Apocrypha the two leaders are "judges" appointed in Babylonia and the prophet Daniel arises to set the record straight. In the Samaritan version the two leaders are men who piously worship on Mount Gerizim, the site of the holy Temple.

In both cases, however, Susannah announces the injustice against her. In the first she appeals to God as "true assessor, righteous judge, and faithful witness." In this way mere human leadership is placed beneath the true justice that God exacts upon people. In the Samaritan version she appeals to God to deliver her from "these two men whose evil instincts are so great that that they have forgotten Your laws." Here again the commandments of men are subordinated to the true judgment of the divine. In that case her father, the priest Rav Amram determines the truth and reveals the falseness of the men. While he has pride of place at the end, however, Susannah is given credit for knowledge of Torah.

In every case, the woman unveils the evil of men who appear as judges or as pious worshipers. Recognizing the feminine critique of male civilizations reveals the weaknesses and inadequacies of a male-centered institutional organization. Woman's spirituality is the touchstone by which to question and advance beyond male claims to an exclusive spirituality. Women do not demand a release from spiritual discipline. Instead they

---

[228] See the discussion of Susannah in James W. Watts, "Ritual Legitimacy and Scriptural Authority," *JBL* 124:3 (Fall 2005), 414.

143

hold up their suspicion of the dominant spirituality as a means of moving to a more rigorous set of spiritual demands.

These stories suggest that society must judge its success or failure by the symptomatic condition of its marginal members. Women stand for a class of people who reveal the flaws within society by illuminating the corruption of government and leadership. Charismatic spirituality takes this corruption as its point of departure. New rules and regulations, new interdicts and obligations, take shape to correct the abuses discovered by investigating the treatment of marginal populations, by uncovering how the oppressed are exploited.

Rabbinic Women and Suspicion of Univocal Decisions

Rabbinic women no less than biblical women often function as critics of male civilization, but in a slightly different way. Two women stand out in particular—Beruriah and Yalta. Yalta flourished during the period of the rabbinic rise to power in Babylonia. That period saw a rising tension between the secular Jewish leadership under the Exilarch and the new power of the rabbinic academies. The conflict between these groups led to the schism of the Karaites and reached its full extent during the time of Saadiah Gaon (882-942).[229] Rabbinic civilizations were

---

[229] See the discussion of the Exilarch and the formation of the rabbinic class throughout Jacob Neusner, *A History of the Jews in Babylonia*. 5 volumes (Leiden: Brill, 1966--1971). Note his contention in volume 4 that "If the Exilarch could not continue to assert his mastery over the rabbis, even in the short run, his administration would be compromised. In the long run, he would have to accept a figurehead status..." 74. On Saadiah see Henry Malter, *Saadiah Gaon: His Life and Works* (Philadelphia: Jewish Publication Society of America, 1921).

coming together and reconciling differences among leading figures. Struggles for authority and with alternate authorities marked the period.

Yalta comes at the beginning of this tension (about the year 250) and negotiates its conflicts.[230] She is said to be the daughter of an Exilarch who has great influence with her rabbinic husband. When she seeks rabbinic counsel she does so in her own way. If one rabbi does not give her the answer that she wants, she goes to another one. She upholds the dignity and equality of women, even at the cost of insulting rabbinic leaders. She even flouts laws of the Sabbath.

At the same time, she supports her husband and affirms his authority. She straddles several civilizations—a civilization granting women equality, one that subjects rabbinic teachings to practical considerations, one that affirms male supremacy and rabbinic authority. By juggling these various civilizations she undermines the claim of any single civilization to be the single *Jewish* civilization. She introduces a charismatic spirituality based on an awareness of the weaknesses in the univocal rabbinic approach. She does not abandon moral or spiritual discipline. Instead she substitutes a feminine spirituality for that of the male establishment.

The figure of Beruriah (first quarter of the second century) is presented far more ambiguously. Much of rabbinic lore speaks of her approvingly. She is the daughter of the martyred Rabbi

---

[230] See the Babylonian Talmud Hullin 109b, 124a, Berachot 51b, Kiddushin 70b, Niddah 20b, Betzah 25b.

Hanina ben Tradyon and the wife of Rabbi Meir. Her knowledge of Talmudic law was considerable, and she even decided legal questions that rabbinic authorities accepted.[231] She wisely keeps the death of her children from her husband throughout the Sabbath so as not to spoil his enjoyment of the holy day and counsels him to accept God's will.[232]

She appears in the Talmud as a biblical exegete. When her husband seeks the death of one of his enemies she provides a counterargument teaching him to read Psalm 104:35 to intend the destruction of sins, not of sinners. When asked by a sectarian to explain a passage in Isaiah 54 she provides an explanation worthy of any rabbinic leader.[233] She even chastises a rabbi for seemingly asking to accompany her on the road—noting that one should not talk with women overmuch![234] Her concern for woman's virtue was extraordinary. When her sister was taken into captivity to become a harlot, Beruriah convinced Rabbi Meir to save her. He succeeded and both he and Beruriah ended up in Babylonia.[235] In

---

[231] Talmud Pesahim 62b'

[232] Midrash Mishlei 31. The story of the death of two children on the Sabbath sometimes appears without Beruriah mentioned at all. See Bin Gorion, *Mimekor Yisrael*, 592--4; The second variant given there eliminates even Rabbi Meir's name. Eli Yassif (*The Hebrew Tale*, 254ff.) notes that a medieval version makes the rabbi the hero who conceals the death of his children from his wife thus rebuilding the tale to eliminate "the controversial Beruriah."

[233] Talmud Berachot 10a.

[234] Talmud Eruvin 53b--54a.

[235] Talmud Avodah Zarah 18a.

all of these, like Yalta, she negotiates between a male centered tradition and woman's equality, creating a sense of skepticism to a civilization developed by rabbinic power.

Later tradition, however, treats her less favorably. One tradition explains Rabbi Meir's flight to Babylonia on the basis of Beruriah's overzealousness for women's dignity. According to this tale, Beruriah objects to the rabbinic teaching that women are lightheaded. Rabbi Meir sought to test her steadfastness and instructed his disciples to try to seduce her. After many failures, they finally succeeded. Beruriah committed suicide in shame, and thus Rabbi Meir had to flee to Babylonia.[236] This tale rejects Beruriah's negotiation between two civilizations and seeks to put her within the single rabbinic, male-dominated, tradition. The need to do this, however, already suggests the effect of her example and influence as a counterforce to a univocal rabbinic civilization. Her alternative spirituality seems to threaten established power.

Tirzah Firestone considers this "Beruriah's Paradox." She succeeds in straddling two civilizations, only to find herself rejected by both. Her story represents what for Firestone is the loss of balance—the choice of one civilization and the rejection of its complement.[237] In another way her story characterizes the Jewish virtue of living among various competing civilizations

---

[236] See Rashi on Avodah Zarah 18b.

[237] See Tirzah Firestone, *The Receiving: Reclaiming Jewish Women's Wisdom* (New York: HarperCollins Publishing, 2003), 52--57; See the entire discussion of Beruriah beginning on p. 42.

and suspecting any civilization claiming exclusivity. Her narrative shows the danger in all totalizing civilizations.

The problem with male-centered civilizations, according to these tales, lies less with their institutional failures than in their silencing of alternative voices. Women seek out divergent readings, raise competing values, and insist upon diversity when faced with civilizations claiming univocal uniformity. A civilization that requires a single cultural standard, that establishes a singular set of rules and regulations, or that allows only one power group a say in governing has forfeited its right to legitimacy.

Charismatic spirituality revitalizes a society by calling attention to the silenced voices of the outcasts and repressed. Listening to those voices requires people to respond to situations they did not know existed. Heeding the call of the disenfranchised entails taking on new duties, fulfilling new obligations. The courage to assert these demands and take them seriously arises from a sympathy and understanding of the suffering that often goes unnoticed. A critic of civilization draws attention to these suppressed voices and the suffering they express. That criticism reminds a community of its own limitations and the way in which its insularity and institutions act against the fullest use of social resources.

Jewish Mystical Civilization and Rabbinic Civilization: A Critique of Apathy

Abraham Joshua Heschel articulated a theology of Judaism deeply influenced by the Jewish tradition. That tradition, however, encompasses several civilizations. Among those, the mystical and the rabbinic had a tense, if often complementary, relationship. Rabbinic Jewish civilization emphasizes the importance of study and the performance of good deeds. It rejects magic and mysticism as alien to Jewish religiousness—there is no "mazal" for Jews—that is they are free from the influence of the celestial bodies.[238] The rabbis may intertwine claims to authority based on scholarship with claims for supernatural power. Nevertheless, their emphasis lies on the power of Torah learning above everything else.

Variants on a common tale show this idea clearly.[239] The story in its earliest form tells how a student sets out to go to the East to learn magic. On his way he stops by what appears to be an inn. Sent out to draw water from a well he descends into an alternate reality, only to return to his original location with the so-called innkeeper asking him why he needs to go to a foreign land when he can stay and study with him, a local magician. This tale includes no disapproval of the search for magical power, just a caution that it can be found close to home rather than far away.

A variant tale (told either about a rabbinic figure or a Hasidic master), however, has the student going to a traditional Jewish leader on his way to learn magic. The rabbi or Hasidic teacher provides the student with an experience of a "long moment" during which the erstwhile magician learns the dangers

---

[238] See the discussion in Yassif, *The Hebrew Folktale*, 162--4.

[239] See Pinhas Sadeh, *Jewish Folktales Selected and Retold by Pinhas Sadeh*. Hillel Halkin, tr. (New York: Doubleday, 1989), 89--92 and Bin Gorion, *Mimekor Yisrael*, 987--8.

of his quest. This magical moment teaches the would-be magical master both the necessity of quitting his search and the greater power of authorized leaders. In this way the hero learns that he does not need alien learning since magic is for non-Jews while Jews have an alternate source of power.

This variant emphasizes that rabbinic teachings while not magical in themselves enable their adherents to surpass the powers of magicians. The dictates of rabbinic laws and behavioral restraints provide the basis for success in life rather than an appeal to the supernatural. A student need not seek out alternative teachers to augment rabbinic lore.

It might appear that since both magicians and rabbinic sages show supernatural powers they should be complementary rather than competitive. In fact, however, they represent different parts of society and different civilizations. The stories of miracle workers during rabbinic times, for example, suggest a tension between rabbinic civilization with its emphasis on study and learning as a source of authority and a mystical one that focuses purely on personal charisma.[240]

One story cycle focuses on the figure of Honi the Circle-Drawer (Babylonian Talmud Taanit 23a).[241] Honi performs

---

[240] See the careful study of this material in Michael D. Swartz, *Scholastic Magic: Ritual and Revelation in Early Jewish Mysticism* (Princeton: Princeton University Press, 1996); compare the discussion of mystical authority as competition to the rabbis in Yassif, *The Hebrew Folktale*, 116--9.

[241] See the discussion in ibid. and the stories reproduced in Bin Gorion, *Mimekor Yisrael*, 278--80.

miracles for the people during a time of drought. While similar tales tell of miracles occurring through the recitation of rabbinic prayers and may have been added to mute the import of this story (See Taanit 24a-25b), Honi employs non-rabbinic measures.[242] Honi clearly imitates the divine power over nature. When a drought appears he first reprimands people for trusting him and not God. When he pleads to God for rain he calls the people ignorant ones who "cannot tell the difference between their Father in Heaven and their father here on earth." When compared with tales of other miracle workers, Honi appears as example of the different models by which rabbis exemplify the divine creativity. He represents a distinctive type of leadership—that of the saint or mystical hero.[243] This alternative leadership type challenges the exclusivity of rabbinic power and thus the civilization associated with it.

Stories of Honi's death seem to indicate a disapproval of both his style and intentions. Although some accounts seek to reconcile Honi to the rabbinic tradition adding details such as his concern for ritual celebration or a disapproval that he stands in the place of God "to stop wars," they agree on the general outlines of the tale. During the contest between the two brothers Hyrcanus and Aristobulus for the combined priesthood and

---

[242] Compare the various stories in the appendix to chapter eight in Joseph Heinemann, *Prayer in the Talmud: Forms and Patterns*. Richard Sarason, tr. (Berlin: Walter De Gruyter, 1977), 208--10.

[243] See Kaufmann Kohler, "Abba Father: Title of Spiritual Leader and Saint, " JQR 13 (1901): 567--80.

kingship, the Judeans following Hyrcanus ask Honi to pray on their account. He refuses to pray for one side or the other and prays "do not let either side prevail for evil, but only for good; for these are Your people and those are Your Priests." Whereupon the "wicked men of Judah" fell upon him and killed him such that "the Lord did not delay His vengeance, for He smote the host of Judah, and a great many people died because of the blood of Honi."[244]

The point seems to be that a reputation for magical power that can alter the natural course of events leads to disaster. Leaders who seek to use such charismatic authority to end war will inevitably come to a tragic end. The need for such alternative figures, however, continues through modern times. Honi appears as a supernatural hero who defends the State of Israel through his magical means in some recent folk narratives.[245]

The stories of Honi and other magic workers offer a critique of normative leadership because that leadership restricts access to certain resources needed for Jewish survival. The magical master has recourse to what the elite consider to be an illicit source of power. The mystical hero goes against the established ruling classes of society because their restrictions impoverish the community and leave it more vulnerable than it would otherwise be. Honi represents an extremist rigor—drawing a circle and standing in its center suggests that he has limited himself even more than tradition requires. He offers this

---

[244] See Bin Gorion, *Mimekor Yisrael*, 278--80.

[245] See Yassif, *The Hebrew Folktale*, 415--8.

charismatic spirituality as a way of coping with extraordinary social and historical challenges. Society requires this charismatic spirituality to augment conventional social organization. Only a more rigorous spirituality can call for reconciliation among feuding members of the community. The lesson here goes beyond that made by women who challenge authority. The new element added is that of special prestige. Only someone who lives beyond the conflicts and special interests of society at large can overcome those conflicts and interests.

Jewish Mystics and Class Consciousness in Civilizational Conflict

The significance of the Kabbalah, the developed mystical tradition, goes beyond its alternative source of authority. It also includes social, political and economic aspects. Jewish mysticism from its very inception valorized the lower classes over the rabbinic hierarchy. The poor and the ignorant appear as heroes in mystical lore in a way that places rabbinic learning in question. Rabbinic civilization has an arrogance and power that often leads to class conflict and the rise of an alternative civilization focused on those marginalized by the learned class. That alternative view insists on more rigorous commitment to Jewish life than even the rabbis demand.

The most consistent irritants of rabbinic civilization have been groups of Pietists or "saints" (*Hasidim*) who have insisted on divergent practices and ethical standards than those of mainstream leaders. Ivan Marcus shows how the early proponents of what has been called "German Pietism" (*Hasidei Ashkenaz*) contrasted their religiousness to that of normative

153

Jewish behavior.[246] Marcus notes that while accepting rabbinic teachings as a point of departure, the Pietists demanded new rituals, new standards, and a different source of authority. This new authority emphasized personal connections and private charisma rather than scholarly ability. One remarkable ritual involved making confession of sins before a Pietist confessor—a ritual certainly resembling that of Roman Catholicism even if not definitely derivative from it.[247] This resemblance suggests the universality of the pietistic approach, a characteristic of many of the tales emerging from this mystical movement.

One of the most exemplary and famous stories illustrating the tension between these German Jewish Pietists and rabbinic leaders tells of a shepherd who would offer humble words of thanksgiving to God, even offering to shepherd God's flock for free if that were needed. An arrogant rabbi overheard the shepherd's prayer and reprimanded him. Instead of his personal prayer, the rabbi taught him the official prayers of the Jewish tradition. The next day, however, the shepherd had forgotten what the rabbi had taught him and was afraid to offer his own prayer. He therefore remained silent. The rabbi dreamed that he was brought before the heavenly tribunal because he had robbed God of a dear prayer. The rabbi returned to the shepherd and authorized him to continue using his private worship. This story

---

[246] See Ivan Marcus. *Piety and Society: The Jewish Pietists of Medieval Germany* (Leiden: E.J. Brill, 1981).

[247] Ibid., 75--76, 82.

has universal appeal, reminding people of many traditions, not just Jews, that official leaders often lack the sympathy and understanding necessary when dealing with commoners.[248]

The story not only shows that God desires the heart rather than the outward forms of prayer. More significantly it attacks the rabbinic class as being insensitive and unable to appreciate true prayer when it occurs (much as the priest Eli could not comprehend Hannah's heartfelt prayer). In this way the story does more than just emphasize the common ideal of German Pietism—that of a profound personal connection with the divine and a deep sense of sin and repentance. It also shows a restlessness with the rabbinic authorities of the time. Self-restraint rather than the imposed restraints of external powers expresses true spirituality. The restless search for new forms of renunciation and spirituality characterized the spirituality of the movement and led to so-called "excesses" of asceticism.

Eventually that charismatic spirituality was muted as the established leadership began to include Pietists in its midst. As

---

[248] See the following: Bin Gorion, *Mimekor Yisrael*, 1259; Ivan Marcus, "The Devotional Ideals of Ashkenazic Pietism," in *Jewish Spirituality: From the Bible Through the Middle Ages*. Arthur Green, tr. (New York: Crossroad, 1986), 363; Yassif, *The Hebrew Folktale*, 290--1 (where he claims that after appearing first in *Sefer Hasidim* it "becomes one of the most common of Jewish folktales" and was used in "the controversy within the religious and social leadership of the community.") and 385 where he cites the story in full. Yoav Elstein discusses the influence of this tale on Polish Hasidism and its repercussions in Hasidic tales in his *Maaseh Hoshev : Studies in Hasidic Tales* (Jerusalem: 1983), 24--29. The tale also occurs in the Islamic tradition and Rumi includes it in his *Masnavi*. See Arthur J. Arberry, tr., *Tales From the Masnavi* (Richmond: Curzon Press, 1993; reprint of 191), 132--4.

155

Marcus remarks, later Pietists might agree upon the "path to personal salvation" but they disagreed about how to bring people to that path. While the early Pietists rejected normative social leadership, the later ones became accommodated to it.[249] They merged their Pietistic civilization with the civilization of the rabbis and thereby overcame the tension that had impelled a type of "creative trespass" against the normative power. Jews learned from the mystics to suspect all claims to exclusive piety based on learning or official authorization. Mystics taught them that rabbinic civilization itself was not immune to spiritual blindness. The popularity of a mystic comes less from a supposed relaxation of rabbinic law than to the reinstatement of that law associated with a more rigorous pietism than the rabbis had either imagined or demanded.

The class-consciousness evident in the German Pietists also appears in the *Zohar*. That classic mystical text focuses its criticism on two leadership groups—the aristocratic philosophers and rationalists, on the one hand, and the rabbinic authorities on the other.[250] A representative tale found in several variations throughout the *Zohar* contrasts the wisdom of a precocious youth to the false piety of rabbinic leaders (see *Zohar* I: 238b, III: 186a-192a).[251] This motif raises several interesting points. The youth

---

[249] See Marcus, *Piety and Society*, 11--15.

[250] See the analysis given by Yitzhak Baer, "Mysticism and Social Reform," *A History of the Jews in Christian Spain I.* Louis Schoffman, tr. (Philadelphia: JPSA, 1966), 243--305.

[251] Daniel C. Matt translates the relevant texts and provides commentary on this motif in his Translation and Introduction. *Zohar: The Book of Enlightenment.*

confounds the rabbis who cannot comprehend what he says. The youth's mother asks whether he has tested the rabbis, and he replies that he has and that they have failed the test. The youth not only shows that he knows Jewish law better than the rabbis but that he also can perceive how they have transgressed certain commandments.

At the end of this sequence, the putative author of the *Zohar*, Rabbi Shimon Bar Yochai, announces that a youth of such power cannot stay long in the world. Given the power of the established leadership, the mystical protest seems doomed to failure (*Zohar* III:192a). The precociousness of youth reminds people of obligations and expectations they have forgotten because of established practice and convention. While the movement may be doomed to failure, the mystic succeeds in awakening renewed spiritual consciousness.

Charismatic Spirituality and Social Transformation

A mystical movement avoids failure either by capitulating to the established power group as did the German Pietists or by changing the social order itself. The same dynamic of opposition eventuating in collaboration occurred with a later pietistic movement, that of Polish Hasidism.[252] That movement, however,

---

Preface by Arthur Green. The Classics of Western Spirituality (New York: Paulist Press, 1983), 170--4.

[252] See the entire discussion in Stephen Sharot, *Messianism, Mysticism, and Magic: A Sociological Analysis of Jewish Religious Movements* (Chapel Hill: University of North Carolina Press, 1982), especially "Millenarianism and Mysticism in Eighteenth--Century Poland," 130--54; "Hasidism and the Routinization of Charisma," 155--88.

began in a time of transition, a period in which modernity created a new environment with which Jews would necessarily have to contend. The ultimate success of the movement lies in the fact that the world had altered from that of the rabbinic leaders. The new expectations and obligations they provided for Jews answered questions that had not been asked before but that became endemic during modernity.

Many of the teachings of this modern mystical tradition reach back to earlier sources. Polish Hasidism builds upon inherited ideas, stories, and concepts. Nevertheless, its primacy emphasis lies in creating a new social system. Arthur Green points out that the communal structure of the time, the *kahal* system, was troubled. People had lost trust in the leadership and questioned the validity of the tradition. Hasidism offered an alternative social organization that could legitimate Jewish life.[253] This alternative, of course, straddled a variety of social tensions.

Polish Hasidism reflected several different conflicts and strains within the social order. The conflict involved competing elite groups, disaffection between the elite and the plebeians, one commercial group against another, and even among the poor themselves.[254] This variety has significance because the founder

---

[253] See the discussion in "Typologies of Leadership and the Hasidic Zaddiq," in Arthur Green, ed., *Jewish Spirituality: From the Sixteenth Century Revival to the Present* (New York: Crossroad, 1986), 128--9.

[254] See Moshe Rosman, *Founder of Hasidism: A Quest for the Historical Ba'al Shem Tov* (Berkeley, CA: University of California Press, 1996), 93.

158

of Hasidism is associated with all strata of society and reflects a general malaise rather than a single contention against rabbinic civilization. Above all it expresses a spirituality that makes new demands for piety and requires more, not less, rigor in Jewish living.

The stories about Rabbi Israel Baal Shem Tov reflect the problems of society and the need to transgress boundaries to solve those problems. As a new type of hero he appears sometimes as representative of the masters and sometimes as advocate of outcasts. Several stories tell how the Besht served the masters of his generation. He traveled from one rabbi to another, studying and learning their teachings. He never stayed long with any of these teachers. In his service of these masters, however, he revealed both his own superiority to them and their insufficiencies.[255] Beyond his service to others, however, he earned a title for himself that revealed his true nature.

The term "Baal Shem" means, literally, "Master of the Name." Used of miracle workers, it implies a magical mastery of certain demonic powers, who must serve those who know their names. Many such magicians sprung up during the time of the rise of Hasidism. Rabbi Israel followed in this tradition. He possessed a particularly powerful name the "Shem Tov," the "Good Name," that of the divinity itself. Another way of interpreting the title, however, applies the adjective "good" not to the name but to the man: he was a "good" Baal Shem, a wonder

---

[255] See the various tales in Israel Jacob Klapholtz, *All the Stories of the BESHT* [Hebrew] (Bnai Brak: Mishor, 1969), Volume 2, 48--50.

worker who acted for the benefit of his followers. A final interpretation suggests the term "shem tov" by itself may be translated as "good repute." The Baal Shem Tov is, therefore, a person of good reputation. Rabbi Israel possesses a good name of his own; his power stems from his personality.

The Besht continues a tradition of his predecessors but adds a touch that shows the weakness in the rabbinic civilization. Several stories show that he provides people with amulets that protect them from danger. The variant forms of this story show that at times it emphasized the Besht's power of magical coercion and his skill at defeating others who practiced similar arts.[256]

Perhaps most startling of all, however, is the variant that claims that the Besht discovered this mode of amulet writing from one of his predecessors--Rabbi Naftali HaCohen. The Besht hears that Rabbi Naftali's amulets have great power. He inspects them and finds that they contain only Rabbi Naftali's name. At that point the Besht decides to imitate this practice. From this story a reader can infer that those who oppose the Besht and his magic are not only estranged from the common person but also from the elite scholarly class represented by Rabbi Naftali.

In this vein Hasidic tradition delights in recording the hostility with which the Baal Shem Tov's brother-in-law, Rabbi Gershom, initially misunderstood and resisted the message of Hasidism, only subsequently to be transformed into an ardent disciple. Describing the self-revelation of the Besht, Hasidic

---

[256] Ibid., Volume 1, 236--8.

sources tell how a nameless disciple of Rabbi Gershom, traveling to his master, was forced to stop at the Besht's inn. Even the piety of the Besht's wife could not relieve his sense of restlessness. Compelled by strange circumstances to stay the Sabbath with the Besht, he discovered the Besht's secret and became the emissary of the Besht to the "sect of the Great Hasidim."[257]

Other, similar tales, suggest that many scholars came to test the Besht and ended up being his disciples. In every case he shows that he knows the law as well as they do but that he has spiritual insights that go beyond theirs.[258] The Besht exemplifies charismatic spirituality by exceeding the requirements of ordinary spiritual life. His personalistic religiousness suited the needs of modern Jews seeking a meaningful piety than had previous rabbinic teachings. This emphasis on having a personal relationship with the divine and through a sympathetic leader became successful because it helped Jews cope with the temptations and problems of living in a modern world. It reminded Jews of their heritage even in the face of the modern challenge.

Perhaps the most significant tale that shows how Polish Hasidism undermined traditional practices while affirming a modernistic religiousness tells of an ignorant lad who attends Yom Kippur services with his father. The boy is restless during

---

[257] See Dan Ben Amos and Jerome R. Mintz, eds., *Shivhei HaBesht: In Praise of the Baal Shem Tov* (Bloomington: Indiana University Press, 1970), 28--31.

[258] See Klapholtz, *All The Stories*, Volume 4, 123--55.

the service. He doesn't understand the Hebrew or know the ritual. He does, however, know that he is to show his devotion to God and his desire to serve the divine. As the service comes to a close, the boy cannot remain still. He takes a small pipe that he keeps with him and blows a sharp whistle. At that point the Besht is said to have proclaimed that because of that heartfelt call, all the prayers that had been uttered could finally enter heaven. Without it, they would have remained chained to earthly desires.[259]

The story celebrates the power of alternative prayer, of ritual that arises spontaneously rather than within a legalist context. Whether or not the purpose of the story is to criticize such law, it does have and has been understood to have such an effect. Later variations on the tale have the boy shouting out or crying aloud. Some have him imitating a cockerel and crying "Kukuriku." [260] In this way the tension between normative practice and spiritual expression has been neutralized. Such neutralization, however, again and again needs to be challenged and tension allowed to surface once again. Even in its most normative form, however, the story clearly implies a spirituality that transcends ordinary rabbinic piety.

---

[259] The story is told often and linked to the story of the ignorant shepherd in the tradition of the German Hasidim. See Yassif, *The Hebrew Folktale*, 386--8. Pinhas Sadeh tells the story in *Jewish Folktales*, 396, and gives it an extended analysis, 412--21. He calls it "one of the best known" Jewish tales but denies that it is meant to criticize the social order.

[260] Elstein, *Maaseh Hoshev*, 12.

While rabbinic Judaism stresses obedience to legal teachings, Hasidism replaces this emphasis with a valorization of personal piety, of the expression of private feelings. As Heschel realized, while Jewish law is the "precondition" for the "ultimate redemption of all men" it is also not the most pressing question of the moment. Before turning to law, people need to respond to a personal call, to the demand made upon them to act responsibly.[261] Class tension becomes less important here than the primary significance of dedication and personal commitment to religious actions.

Polish Hasidism moved from social protest to a reconsideration of religious priorities. The criticism of the religious establishment, while retaining an awareness of social inequalities, focused more on how religion had lost its compelling power. Heschel made the same criticism of religion in contemporary life. He claimed that it had declined because it was "irrelevant, dull, oppressive, insipid."[262] This echoes the lesson of Polish Hasidism. Charismatic spirituality erupts from a discontent with ordinary spirituality, with the routinization of religious life. The need for new interdicts and more rigorous expectations comes not only through criticizing authoritarian leadership, the silencing of marginal voices, or the inequalities of the economic structure. The insensitivity of religious traditions to a transformed world and the new demands it makes also requires a critical response. Being aware that religion has failed becomes the

---

[261] Heschel, *Insecurity*, 216--20.

[262] Idem., *God In Search of Man*, 3.

163

foundation for a charismatic spirituality that revives religious commitment.

CHAPTER SIX:

Heschel, Ritual and Charismatic Spirituality

Ritual in the Thought of Abraham Joshua Heschel

Abraham Joshua Heschel had little patience for "ritual" or ceremonial religion. He agreed with the prophets who rejected the priests with their call for ceremonies rather than justice, whose piety "was fraud and illusion."[263] Ritualistic actions distract people from the important theme of religion—answering the call to action and righteousness. Too often what Heschel calls "episodes of spiritual rhapsody" substitute for responsibility.[264]

Nevertheless, deeds that could be called ritual action are given positive evaluation in his work, and they illustrate the four virtues adumbrated in previous chapters. Ritual offers an opportunity to respond to the God whose demands call us forth into personhood. Ritual points to the lessons of history—to the nightmare of human events and to the Messianic promise against which they must be judged. Ritual changes in response to diverse cultural environments; these changes reflect the generosity of sharing with others and accepting what others share with you. Finally the crisis of ritual suggests the need to question

---

[263] Abraham Joshua Heschel, *The Prophets* (Philadelphia: Jewish Publication Society, 1962), 11.

[264] Abraham Joshua Heschel, *Man is Not Alone: A Philosophy of Religion* (New York: Farrar, Straus and Giroux, 1951), 289.

165

civilization, to be skeptical of the structures of contemporary society. While Heschel may oppose the category of "ritual," he recognizes that Jewish practices help renew spirituality.

In contrast to the term "ritual", Heschel offers the category of "mitzvah," commandment. He defines rituals and symbols as human inventions. He considers them expressions of ideas, references to what people believe about the divine. They substitute intellectual constructs for a living religious response. In that way, he dismisses such ceremonies as "the homage which disbelief pays to faith."[265] Nevertheless he affirms traditional Jewish practice, defining it as mitzvah, a commandment that presents an opportunity for a person to share the divine concern, to stand with God and respond to the deity's demand. In this way it enhances personhood. Standing "with God" entails recalling the divine pathos, remembering those emotional patterns deeply embedded in the structures of life.

To become a person means to hear a demand addressed to you, Heschel avers. A mitzvah is a response to that demand. Ritual, understood as mitzvah, is not an attempt to reach God nor a means of teaching the love of God. Instead it enhances the love of responding to God, the desire to answer a call.[266] In striving to fulfill this type of response, a person actualizes inner potential. The goal of ritual observance understood as mitzvah, he claims,

---

[265] Abraham Joshua Heschel, *Man's Quest for God: Studies in Prayer and Symbolism* (New York: Charles Scribner's Sons, 1954), 114.

[266] Ibid., 123.

is self-transformation; its success lies in transforming people, allowing them to transcend the merely human.[267]

Heschel contends that Jewish religion consists, above all else, in the creation of a view of reality, a sense of the order of existence. Those who see Jewish practice as a ritualistic regimen have misunderstood it, according to Heschel. He remarks that "the order of Jewish living is meant to be, not a set of rituals, but an order of all of man's existence."[268]

Rituals are more than tools for personal development. They remind those who perform them of the significance of the whole of life, of the meaning of reality. Rituals become mitzvoth when seen as "essentially attempts to remove our callousness to the mystery of our own existence and pursuits."[269] Rituals correctly practiced draw attention to a call to action through which we become a self. Understood as mitzvah, these actions bring people into contact with the responsibility that defines them and their answer to the challenges of their lives.

While Heschel sees religious observance as an opportunity to respond to a divine call, as a way to become a responsive person, he also recognizes the effect of these actions as reminders of history. History provides moments of illumination, moments in which the nightmare of human events becomes clear and

---

[267] Abraham Joshua Heschel, *God In Search of Man: A Philosophy of Judaism* (New York: Farrar, Straus, and Cudahy, 1955), 311.

[268] Heschel, *Man's Quest For God*, 106.

[269] Heschel, *God In Search of Man*, 63.

167

moments in which the promise of the future offers a hope and inspiration. Heschel declares that both history and ritual provide a "sanctuary in time," a way of coming to grips with historical suffering, of inspiring compassion.

Entering the sanctuary of the Sabbath, for example, people realize the sterility of their ordinary lives and are called on a pilgrimage to the messianic.[270] Experiencing the power of the Sabbath recalls people to themselves. They compare this peace to the turmoil of daily existence. They see the nightmare of everyday living. It is this aspect of ritual that enables Heschel to say that true worship, ritual truly oriented toward responsiveness, teaches compassion. Not only does ritual performance understood as mitzvah enhance the quality of people's life, it also teaches them to care for others.[271]

Heschel also recognizes that ritual observance differs from one historical period to another—that God, the partner who calls for human action by filling the universe with cues for positive human emotions, uses different means to energize a love of justice at different times. He notes that the early rabbinic leaders lived in a context that made exalted spirituality possible. Not all people at all times can achieve that level of commitment. The

---

[270] Heschel declares history itself to be the locus for "sanctuaries in time" in *God In Search of Man*, 423; he discusses the Sabbath as an example of a ritual mitzvah that provides an equally powerful sanctuary throughout his *The Sabbath: Its Meaning for Modern Man*, Expanded Edition (New York: Harper and Row, 1966).

[271] Heschel, *God In Search of Man*, 360.

power to observe, he avows, depends on the situation.[272] He admits that even for those loyal to Jewish law many details and requirements impede rather than enhance a life of obedience and rigor.[273] Ritual understood as commandments or mitzvoth adapts to the needs of different historical realities.

Heschel sees the mitzvoth as "signposts" to the demands made on each person. Those demands change with the situation, and, therefore, signposts differ with differing situations.[274] He insists that Jewish history shows that there are times during which the question is not how much Jews can observe, but how deeply they can live out the commandments that are available to them. The question today is the discovery of which rituals do in fact awaken an awareness of our responsibility for action.[275]

Heschel addressed the possibility of using ritual as a tactic for reminding people of the need to question the status quo. He corrected those who thought that new translations of the prayer book would make prayer more accessible. What Jews needed, he argued, is not new renderings of the words, but translations of the self. The crisis of prayer should teach people to change their hearts and souls not the texts that they read.[276] He announced that

---

[272] Ibid., 303.

[273] Ibid., 302.

[274] Ibid. 426.

[275] Heschel, *Man's Quest For God*, 102.

[276] Ibid., 33, 82--83.

the present period is "one of the great hours of history" because people have recognized that they need to learn how to pray, that ritual action needs a revival of its meaning as mitzvah.[277]

In this way a failure in ritual because it has lost its sense of commandment raises just those questions necessary to challenge civilization, to ask whether the forms and structures of this civil society require change. An unsuccessful ritual experience brings forth just that skeptical attitude toward civilization that inspires charismatic spirituality to demand more rigorous religious living. Because ritual fails, mitzvah once again becomes a possibility for spirituality.

Ritual and the Decline of Civilization: Gershom Scholem's Tale

What appears as the same ritual experience may, in fact, take on different guises, sometimes appearing as a salutary failure and sometimes as a cautionary success. Heschel looks particularly at normative Jewish rituals. Jews have, however, created alternative rituals as well. These rituals may well show how any ritual process exemplifies the virtues necessary for charismatic spirituality. This point becomes clear when examining a late Hasidic story about ritual and how interpreters view its experience. The variety of interpretations shows the multifaceted nature of any ritual process.

Gershom Scholem concluded his study of *Major Trends in Jewish Mysticism* by repeating a story presented by the novelist

---

[277] Ibid., xiii.

S. Y. Agnon.[278] The story traces the way a Hasidic hero, the Baal Shem Tov, created a ritual that later followers tried to imitate but could not. He uses it to conclude his survey of the history of Jewish mysticism as a means of illustrating the condition of Judaism, or at least of Jewish mysticism, currently. He claims that the story is ambivalent–some interpreters would say "it symbolizes the decay of a great movement" but it can also be said that "it reflects the transformation of all its values." In either case, Scholem interprets the story optimistically but cautiously: " the story is not ended, it has not yet become history, and the secret life it holds can break out tomorrow in you or in me."[279] This statement suggests hope for future spirituality.

Scholem does not claim that ritual has been replaced by the telling of stories. Instead, he intimates that telling stories is itself a powerful ritual, a ritual that can transform both the storyteller and the audience. Story is not mere theory but deed: "Nothing at all has remained theory, everything has become a story." Far from averring that by becoming story ritual has atrophied, Scholem argues that story is itself a ritual act that goes beyond theory and plays an active role in shaping Jewish life.[280] The story challenges the belief that a transvaluation of ritual alters its

---

[278] Gershom G. Scholem, *Major Trends in Jewish Mysticism* (New York: Schocken, 1961), 349--50. This section revises some material from my "Rethinkng Jewish Ritual: Toward an Eclectic Approach," *Arc: The Journal of the Faculty of Religious Studies*, McGill University, Montreal, Canada 27 (1999): 67--78.

[279] Scholem, *Major Trends*, 350.

[280] Ibid., 350.

power. Each change in the ritual challenges the conviction that only materialistic culture solves problems.

To make this point, Scholem restructures and remolds Agnon's original tale. According to Scholem's version, the Besht originally carried out a specific routine whenever he had "a difficult task before him." He would go to a special place, light a fire, and meditate in prayer. When all these actions are completed, then the task that needed to be done has been accomplished, reality has been altered to fit the needs of the Besht. Thus place, action, and prayer are the central elements in achieving a certain goal. The decline comes as one after another of these elements becomes inaccessible. First, the specific actions associated with the routine are forgotten, but the place and the prayers are remembered. Then the prayers are lost, but the sacred place is recalled. In each case, however, that which needed to be achieved is finally accomplished. Eventually not even the place is remembered but the story seems to have "the same effect as the actions of the other three."

The sequence has an important significance in understanding the story. By making place the final part of the ritual to be lost, the tale makes it the most important. The key idea is that ritual involves a change of place and that telling stories may effect a type of metaphysical dislocation that corresponds to the geographical change of place indicated in the tale itself.

Ritual, according to the story itself, transforms reality by a transformation of place. Change of place intimates a criticism of life as ordinarily lived. It offers a critique of civilization and engenders skepticism. A difficult task need not be carried out in exactly the same way in every case. The key to success in that task lies less in its details than in transforming civilization, in moving from ordinary place to extraordinary. Ritual—whether elaborate or merely storytelling—creates changes by showing new possibilities despite the reality of present civilization.

The displacements throughout the story reinforce the idea of a criticism of civilization and the demand for change. Fire in a forest presents both an enigmatic and dangerous intrusion of the human into the natural. Although humanity has tamed much of the destructive power of fire, reintroducing that element into the woods suggests recklessness, as the cliché "playing with fire" discloses. In Scholem's telling of this tale, the precarious use of a domesticated power within a wild setting represents the most extreme example of ritual power.

The next aspect of ritual to be lost is the special meditation used by the Besht. Here again the social and conventional has been displaced into the natural and untamed. Prayer is most often associated with public worship, with devotion in the midst of community. Even when practiced in private, prayer usually seeks to impose discipline and order on the mind. Here, however, prayer takes flight in the midst of a primeval forest. It is taken out of its communal or structured setting and, like fire, returned in its pristine dangerous form, to the wilds.

The place itself, then, becomes the sign and signal of the transformation that occurs. To go to the place means to return *ab origine* to the fount of one's beginnings, to the primitive roots of humanity's development. This aspect of the tale represents charismatic spirituality as a reminder of those duties and obligations often forgotten in the "routinization" of ritual, in the transformation of what once was extraordinary to what is commonplace.

How then does telling a story perform the same function and achieve the same end? Perhaps because it eschews intellectualization and theory, storytelling recalls the primitive impulse of thought itself, an impulse best expressed in narrative and only later tamed and subdued into theoretical shape. As retold by Scholem, then, the Hasidic narrative about the decline in generations demonstrates the necessity of going back to origins. Ritual represents a regression to original immediacy–to fire without civilization, to prayer without a community, to a place without human interference, to words without intellectual structure. Such an approach might appear as "therapeutic," as a relaxation of cultural restraints. Instead, however, it represents the prelude to renewed commitment to original duties and obligations.

Heschel's view, echoed by Scholem in his use of the story of the changing generations of Hasidic leaders, considers ritual not only dispensable but also often an obstacle to faith. Ritual is utilitarian and social, whereas authentic religion is immediate and spontaneous. This view suggests that ritual creates an artificial situation, that it constructs a human framework which believers may infuse with meaning and significance, but which by itself has no dynamic power. Understood in this way, ritual should provide an opportunity for reflecting on religion generally and its inadequacies in particular. Thus the ritual process described by

174

Scholem's story applies to many ritual traditions, not merely those of the Jews.

For many, as Heschel recognized, ritual practice takes on the appearance of a tribute to the past. It reminds people of the inadequacies of the present. At the same time, the rituals still succeed in transforming people's attitudes. They still act to draw attention away from the external trappings of civilization to the natural foundations of all life. Heschel's view of the Sabbath as a time for "opening up new roads for ultimate realizations" applies to Scholem's view of stories and to any person's experience of the transformative power of altered rituals.[281] In this way an experience of even revised ritual can serve to stimulate charismatic spirituality.

Ritual and the Nightmare of History

Not every interpretation of the Hasidic story Scholem adapted expresses this optimistic view—the story may point to a value neglected rather than continuity of personal change. Elie Wiesel, for example, relates the same story but from a far more pessimistic perspective.[282] Scholem affirms the ability of ritual storytelling to fulfill the purposes served by earlier, now abandoned rites, Wiesel disagrees. Wiesel makes the story a tale of declining ritual effectiveness. When a disaster threatens the Jewish people, Wiesel recounts, then a righteous leader, a *Zaddik*,

---

[281] Heschel, *The Sabbath*, 100.

[282] See Elie Wiesel, *Souls On Fire: Portraits and Legends of Hasidic Masters*. Marion Wiesel, tr. (New York: Random House, 1972), 167--8.

performs rites meant to ward it off. Wiesel seems to follow Scholem as the original ritual loses first its magical fire, then its special prayer, and finally the special place. He too relates that at that junction all that was left was the story. Yet Wiesel adds a skeptical note to this tale. Sometimes telling the story fails to achieve the desired aim of the ritual.

This series of successful attempts to counteract danger ends dramatically in the modern period. Wiesel looks at modernity through the prism of the Nazi Holocaust. If ritual were to be effective, then that event should not have occurred. That it did happen undermines the presuppositions of ritual action. Wiesel's conclusion to Agnon's story suggests that the tale cannot continue. At this final point, Wiesel comments,

> And it was sufficient. It no longer is. The proof is that the threat has not been averted. Perhaps we are longer able to tell the story. Could all of us be guilty? Even the survivors? Especially the survivors? [283]

All that remains is not hope but compassion; the story Agnon tells should inspire a sense of responsibility and sympathy. The guilt that Wiesel suggests as the residue left from the tale should awaken compassion for victims of a failed rite.

What lies behind Wiesel's pessimism? He has concluded that the rites and beliefs of the past cannot resolve the issues of the present. Wiesel denies the power and effectiveness of traditional Jewish practices, yet he also does not create new rituals, to affirm the power of symbolism in some altered way.

---

[283] Ibid., 168.

He gives their failure meaning–a personal meaning that illuminates the problems of modern existence. For Wiesel, that entails confronting the overwhelming new responsibility humanity faces. The insufficiency of past ritual forces each human being today to shoulder the duties of saving the world, of averting disaster. Wiesel's theme has become "reliance upon man in a world devoid of God," in a world in which traditions become "significant in allowing a person to face his fate." Ritual confronts each person with the duty to act precisely because ritual fails, because it cannot accomplish now what it once achieved.[284]

From this perspective, ritual, including, and especially, the ritual of storytelling, communicates by its very failure the limitations within which modern people must live. Ritual failure forces a recognition of reality, the reality of a post-Holocaust world. In that new reality, all that remains is a sense of duty, of fellowship among victims, of a compassion that extends to all human beings. The lesson Wiesel draws from this story applies to all ritual failures, not merely that of Jews after the Holocaust. Wiesel's question about the guilt of survivors recalls the phrase running through Heschel's writing that although some are guilty, all are responsible.[285] Ritual causes silence, interrupts intellectual

---

[284] See Michael Berenbaum, *The Vision of the Void : Theological Reflections on The Works of Elie Wiesel* (Middletown, CN: Wesleyan University Press, 1979).

[285] See the discussion in Robert McAfee Brown, "Some Are Guilty, All are Responsible: Heschel's Social Ethics in John C. Merkle, ed., *Abraham Joshua Heschel: Exploring His Life and Thought* (New York: Macmillan, 1985), 123--41, and see, for example, Heschel, *God In Search of Man*, 93.

and theological attempts to make sense of history. It breaks up the routine of living and admonishes philosophy to quiet its ceaseless murmuring. Ritual transforms time and space–breaking up the familiar continuity that both provide for life.

Modern rituals refuse to let history speak for itself. They remind Jews that history is mysterious, unfathomable, beyond the simple explanations and natural understandings of human thinking. The ritual arouses a sense of history's nightmare.

Such a sense of nightmare inspires compassion for the victims of history. The failure of ritual awakens a sympathy for those caught in the vulgarity of technical civilization. Heschel finds in the Sabbath a respite from "external obligations," and the lack of such a rest from history arouses his compassion and care for modern women and men.[286] The absence of such ritual respite leads to his declaration that no other institution "holds out a greater hope for man's progress."[287] What moves Heschel is compassion. Although he speaks only of the Sabbath, his depth of feeling applies to all who experience failed ritual processes. This compassion inspires new ways of acting, new ritual procedures, and an authenticity of religious responsiveness.

---

[286] Heschel, *The Sabbath*, 28.

[287] Ibid.,

Ritual Changes and the Demands of Cultural Context

The tale which both Scholem and Wiesel tell goes back to an original story attributed to the Hebrew novelist, S.Y.Agnon.[288] Agnon's own retelling of the tale reflects the social and cultural reality of European Hasidism, a religious movement in which the role of the leader, the Zaddik is paramount. In his telling of this narrative the element of social or political power advances to the forefront, an element associated with the necessity to accommodate changing cultural conditions As Agnon tells the story, an occasion for *pikuach nefesh*, the saving of a life, occurred when a man's only son faced some unspecified danger. The man and his son came to the Zaddik Israel of Rizhin and asked for help. The Zaddik replied that in the days of the Baal Shem Tov, may his merit guard us (a phrase repeated at the mention of every Zaddik in this tale), just such an event also occurred. The Baal Shem Tov ordered the making of a candle, the taking of the candle into the forest and lighting it by a certain tree, constructing a fire, and doing other sorts of mysterious things there. Then with God's help deliverance was effected.

In the next generation a similar event happened, and the Great Maggid was approached to appeal for mercy. The context had changed; cultural conditions now differed; the Maggid could only accomplish what his new situation allowed. He was able to do all the actions except kindle the mystical fire or recite the

---

[288] See Shmuel Yosef Agnon, *Sefer, Sofer, VeSippur: Sippurim Al Sofrim Veal Sefarim* [Hebrew] (Tel Aviv: Schocken, 1978), 439.

special meditations but by relying on the merit of what the Baal Shem Tov had done, the deliverance was accomplished.

Once more a similar event took place, this time in the days of Rabbi Moshe Leib of Sassov when social and political life was even more drastically transformed. When the supplicants came to him, he went to the special tree and confessed that he did not have the power to do what his predecessors had done. Nevertheless, he continued, he would recite all their deeds before God. He told the entire tale, and by God's help the deliverance was effected. We, however, the Rebbe of Rizhin remarked, do not have the power even to do that much. However, we can tell the tales of the Zaddikim, and God will perform the deed. And, indeed, God did so.

Several points of interest occur in this rendition. First, the significance of place is reduced. What is important is knowing the special tree and performing the special actions there. Holiness of place has given way to a holiness of secret knowledge. The designated actions are also made more complicated and detailed. Fire and candle are distinguished here as two ritual actions. They are less symbolic of some general idea (such as taming the wild) than of performing miraculous actions. Thus lighting a candle may be possible even when kindling a special fire and reciting magical incantations might not be. The wonderous actions the ritual expert performs becomes less and less as time goes on. Jews adapt to their cultural settings; they lose some of what is specifically their own, but also retain a sense of distinctiveness.

Finally, all that remains is the act of conveying the wonder at what earlier generations of leaders could accomplish. While the human audience feels this wonder, the intended audience of the narration is the divine. When God hears what the heroes of the past achieved, then God acts on behalf of their descendants. While Agnon seems to be emphasizing the power inherent in stories, the point is rather that the power of God continues to act despite the change of generations.

These stories suggest that in the face of altered cultural circumstances, God continues to remain faithful. Previous generations offered God different gifts—a special tree, candle, or rite. Now all they can offer is a story. What God requires, however, is only the spirit of generosity. Offering up stories may be just as generous as offering up magical rites or revealing secret prayers. While telling about what Jewish leaders, the Zaddikin, can do, the focus of Agnon's story is what these leaders actually offer to God so that God will respond to them.

Agnon's tale appears limited to Jews. Nevertheless the theme of "saving a life" requires notice. Jewish tradition allows for and even demands extraordinary actions when a human life—all human life whether that of a Jew or Non-Jew--is at stake. In the story this seems to operate on two levels. On one level it suggests that in connection with such a case a leader will use the entire arsenal of magical ritual possible. On another level it suggests that God may well allow a lesser instrument to succeed, even though under ordinary circumstances it might fail, just because of the crucial nature of the situation. Success depends on God's grace, not human actions.

This anthropomorphic view of the divine need not be taken literally. God, understood as the source and stimulus of human

181

emotions, underlies all human actions. As human emotions respond to and create an environment in which people live, they take on a power of their own. The story suggests the value and significance of these emotions, of the way expressing emotional need and addressing emotional issues influences human existence generally. We may think ourselves victims of the emotional environments in which we live. In fact, these are gifts given to us.

That the various rituals at each stage do all succeed does not, therefore, validate the ritual power of those performing them. Rather the success points to God's mercy and leniency, to the positive force of the emotions shaping human life. More than that, the motive involved is just that generosity necessary for charismatic spirituality. Ritual offers an opportunity to show the divine an intention to share with others and offer oneself for them. As Agnon tells the story the cultural element is deemphasized. Generosity appears only in the Zaddik's answer and in the call for *pikuach nefesh*, a concern that Jewish law applies to the lives of human beings generally, not just members of the Jewish community. Nevertheless, cultural diversity appears as an inevitable background to the story. Such diversity provides the context in which the divine answers humanity and humanity appeals to the divine. Every human community shares with every other one tactics for channeling and using emotional resources for the good of humanity.

Heschel emphasizes that Judaism has as its goal not merely the elevation of Jews but rather of "being a source of spiritual wealth, a source of meaning relevant to all peoples."[289] One lesson that all can learn from Jews is the necessity for generosity, for sharing and offering what one has to another. In the story the leaders offer their expertise to God. This symbolizes using personal talents to answer the demands arising from a certain situation. When life is in danger, people with ability must draw on all resources to give protection from that danger. Charismatic spirituality entails building new obligations and expectations from the cultural expressions available. The generosity of cultural exchange provides the raw material out of which that spirituality derives its effectiveness and power.

Ritual And The Responsive Self

Agnon's version of the story of the declining generations inspired Scholem and Wiesel even as they altered many details from his version. Moshe Idel takes a closer, more scholarly, look at Agnon's use of his sources.[290] As with Scholem, and unlike Wiesel or Agnon, Idel considers the tale not one of decline and loss but of continued efficacy. More than that, he seems to consider it a proof of spiritual advancement. Idel comments that "If there is a decline, it is in the knowledge of theurgy, which is, however, complemented by a direct address to God....The loss of theurgy...is compensated by the discovery of forms of personal

---

[289] Abraham Joshua Heschel, *The Insecurity of Freedom: Essays on Human Existence* (New York: Farrar, Straus and Giroux, 1966), 226.

[290] Moshe Idel, *Kabbalah: New Perspectives* (New Haven: Yale University Press, 1988), 270--1, 397 n.96).

mysticism."[291] The tale, as he reads it, relates how private piety displaces magical practices. The abandonment of external rituals led to a higher type of religiousness, that of private devotion.

Idel tends to follow the lead of Agnon in the details that he brings in contrast to both Scholem and Wiesel. Nevertheless, the text that Idel reproduces has several differences from the retellings in other settings. Idel's source, like Agnon's version of the tale, describes how the Rabbi Rizhin was asked to "save the life" of the son of one of his followers. The story, then, concerns neither a "difficult task" nor "disaster" threatening the Jewish people. It is a matter of *pikuach nefesh*—the saving of a soul.

Unlike Agnon, Idel emphasizes the individual nature of this purpose and its universalism. He does not focus on the obligation to save lives, but on the significance of the "soul" of an individual. This emphasis on the individual's spiritual self provides Idel with his point of departure. The Rabbi of Rizhin then describes what the Besht performed and the changes made by his successors. The Besht, in this story, goes to a forest and takes a special candle that he attaches to a special tree that stands alone—this version never mentions the mention of making a fire. Idel interprets both the candle and the trees as referring to the soul of the son whose life is in danger.

The attachment of the son's soul to the "tree of souls" is, for Idel, an example of "sympathetic magic." In later developments that magic is replaced by the more psychological

---

[291] Ibid., 271.

tie between the individuals involved and the divine; direct action replaces symbolic rite.[292] For Idel, ritual provides the opportunity for personal development, for a response to a call directed to the individual and requiring an answer. Idel construes the development of the narrative as a story of how, in every case, whatever the ritual accompaniments involved, the essential act is that of an individual's piety.

Of striking significance in Idel's sources is the absence of an emphasis on place or even the detail of specific actions. While the figure of the special tree remains in Idel's telling of the first two cases of effective intervention, its neglect is not considered significant. The Besht is said to have attached the special candle to the special tree and done various meditations, but the specific actions play no real role in what follows. The author relates that the first generation after the Besht did "as mentioned above" but declared, "since the special prayers of the Baal Shem Tov are not known to me, I shall do this on the basis of the *kavanah* which the Besht intended." He, too, was received favorably by God and the deliverance was accomplished.

The final generation claimed, "We do not even have the power to do that, but I shall only tell the story to God so that he will help." And, indeed, the story concludes, God did help. The intense devotion of the Zaddik replaced the expertise of former leaders.[293]

---

[292] Ibid., 397, n.94.

[293] Ibid., 270--1; other versions, however, merely have "I shall tell the story (no audience specified), and God will help." See Israel Jacob Klapholtz, *All the Sto*

According to this version, the specific elements that brought about the deliverance are irrelevant. The Besht uses extraordinary actions (the mention of the candle here is unique, despite Idel's desire to connect it with a memorial candle lit for a close relative) and recites extraordinary prayers. The next generation enacts the same mystic deeds but forgoes the prayers. Finally, neither extraordinary prayer nor extraordinary deed is really required. All that is really necessary is an appeal to the divine, and even without all the external rituals, God will answer such a cry. God's compassion to the personality of the worshiper is central. God saves a soul because that soul has reached out to the divine and responded to the voice it hears.

The common element at every stage is God taking action for the sake of human beings. The various stages in the story represent different ways in which individuals seek God. Idel's presentation of the Hasidic story emphasizes that differences among individuals in their approaches to the divine have little significance. The human self can assume various forms in its attunement to God. Ritual merely provides an external expression of an inner conviction and trust. In this way, the story affirms the fact of human difference, of the right of people to change themselves, to evolve through time, and to remain faithful even if they appear to be doing new things.

Ritual exists as an extension of the human self, and as the self grows and develops, so too ritual must develop. Rituals that remain unchanging are unfaithful to the reality of God's

ries of the BESHT, vol. 3 [Hebrew] (Bnai Berak: Mishor, 1989), 43--44.

demands. This means that ritual acts must reflect the reality of the individual, in all the changing dynamism of a developing self. As the self undergoes development, new rituals must emerge to awaken the self to new opportunities for spiritual growth.

Heschel recognized this aspect of religious practice. He emphasized that all depends on "the inner attitude."[294] He identifies the purpose of prayer as transforming the individual. From "self-consciousness" prayer initiates the worshiper into "self-surrender." In this way prayer becomes a "personal duty" and not just a communal ceremony.[295] This sense of duty creates a responsive personality, a personality sometimes ambitious and sometimes humble, but always willing to answer the call that it hears, a call that brings forth new interdicts and new demands. Thus prayer as personal engagement with the divine leads to creative spirituality.

Ritual and the Values of Charismatic Spirituality

How does ritual lead to charismatic spirituality? Depending on how one experiences it, ritual may reinforce one or another of the virtues essential for charismatic spirituality. The variety of interpretations of ritual offered culminate in the caution against too great a reliance on ritual itself. Religious spirituality arises from a religious practice that points beyond itself to some greater concern. That concern might be one of generosity—seeking to save a human life provides one such example. The concern might

---

[294] Heschel, *Insecurity* 232.

[295] Heschel, *Man's Quest For God*, 55--57.

be to inspire the abandonment of ritual as the prelude to a more creative set of expectations and obligations.

Another concern might be for a recognition of individual differences and the affirmation of the value of those differences. Ritual abandonment often offers a more profound gauge of religious commitment than its retention. In other cases, ritual action may appear as a poor substitute for genuine religious experience and point the need for spiritual renewal. No single hermeneutic for decoding symbolic actions encompasses all the possible meanings and uses of ritual, whether Jewish or non-Jewish. By refusing to universalize a single theory of ritual, students of religious practice may attain a clearer vision of both the purposes of ritual and of the opportunities granted for charismatic spirituality.

The ritual analyzed here—one designed for a specific purpose and not part of the regular calendar of rituals—reveals several depth-theological elements. Behind the external actions which manifest the particularity of the rite, stand general concepts relevant to all religious expressions.

Both the examples given here and throughout this book and Heschel's own writing draw upon the data of Judaism. Nevertheless, study of that data uncovers a more general urge behind the particularity of the examples. In every case the experience that eventually takes shape as a Jewish expression originates in a universal value. Sometimes that value springs from a recognition that the human self develops in response to a personal call. Sometimes the virtue affirmed arises from ritual experienced as having failed and having lost its power thus engendering greater compassion. Other times the virtue associated with the ritual derives generosity from its shared cultural context, and at still other times it comes from the inculcation of a skeptical attitude toward civilization.

In each of these cases ritual points beyond itself to the purpose of religious life more generally. Ritual is characterized as mitzvah or commandment. Abraham Joshua Heschel contends that in the performance of such a deed a person becomes a symbol of the divine. Human beings do not need to "have" symbols but rather to "be a symbol," a symbol of God.[296] As noted throughout this book, references to divinity take on different meaning for different people. The story of the transformation of ritual analyzed here exemplifies this diversity.

God takes on several guises in religious life. God may refer to the source of those spiritual demands calling forth the personal response upon which an authentic personality depends. The term may also stand for the origin of that sense of outrage and extraordinary shame humans feel inexorably when faced with the horrors of history. Divine pathos may refer to the foundation of that compassion with which one person looks upon the suffering of others. God as concerned for all humanity may point toward the human impulse for borrowing from other cultures and sharing with them. Seeing pluralism as a divinely created opportunity allows people to interact with generosity. Finally judging any civilization from a divine rather than human perspective recognizes the validity of discontent, the legitimacy of skepticism

---

[296] Ibid., 126.

not merely of this one civil order but of any humanly constructed society. The religious life develops out of a response to all these different guises of the divine. The renewed set of expectations and obligations that are the hallmark of charismatic spirituality point backwards to the divine source and thereby binding together these varied sources of charismatic spirituality.

SELECTED BIBLIOGRAPHY

Note that this is a selected bibliography focused on the main themes of this book. Secondary works on Heschel can be found throughout the footnotes and have been omitted here. Throughout this work, particularly in the footnotes, a careful reader will notice the writings of the philosopher Leo Strauss. Although I cannot find a justification for a special section of this bibliography devoted to his works, an interested reader should turn to the cited references in the footnotes for enlightenment and understanding.

I. Abraham Joshua Heschel

"The Mystical Element in Judaism," in *The Jews* II, Louis Finkelstein, ed. (Philadelphia: Jewish Publication Society of America, 1949. Pp. 602-23.

Man is Not Alone: A Philosophy of Religion. New York: Farrar, Straus and Giroux, 1951.

Mans Quest for God: Studies in Prayer and Symbolism. New York: Charles Scribner's sons, 1954.

God In Search of Man: A Philosophy of Judaism. New York: Farrar, Straus and Cudahy, 1955.

Theology of Ancient Judaism [Hebrew]. London: Soncino, 1962.

The Prophets. Philadelphia: Jewish Publication Society, 1962.

The Insecurity of Freedom: Essays on Human Existence. New York: Farrar Straus and Giroux, 1966.

A Passion For Truth. New York: Farrar, Straus and Giroux, 1973.

Moral Grandeur and Spiritual Audacity: Essays Edited by Susannah Heschel. New York: Farrar, Straus, and Giroux, 1996.

II. Jewish Folktales

Ben-Yehezkiel, Mordekhai. *Sefer Ha-Ma'Asiyot* [Hebrew]. Volume 6. Tel Aviv: Devir, 1957.

Bin Gorion, Micah Joseph. *Mimekor Yisrael: Classical Jewish Folktales.* Emanuel bin Gorion, ed. I.M.Lask, tr. Bloomington: Indiana University Press, 1976.

Sadeh, Pinhas. *Jewish Folktales Selected and Retold by Pinhas Sadeh.* Hillel Halkin, tr. New York: Doubleday, 1989.

Schwartz, Howard. *Tree of Souls: The Mythology of Judaism.* New York: Oxford University Press, 2004.

Yassif, Eli. *The Hebrew Folktale: History, Genre, Meaning.* Jacqueline S. Teitelbaum, tr. Forward Dan Ben Amos Bloomington: Indiana University Press, 1999.

III. Judaism, Religion and Spirituality

Buxbaum, Yitzhak Israel. *Storytelling and Spirituality in Judaism.* Northvale, NJ: Jason Aronson, 1994.

Dan, Joseph. *On Sanctity: Religion, Ethics and Mysticism in Judaism and Other Religions* [Hebrew]. Jerusalem: Magnes Press, 1997.

Eliade, Mircea. *Patterns in Comparative Religion*. Rosemary Sheed, tr. (New York: Sheed and Ward, 1958.

Frolich, Mary. "Spiritual Discipline, Discipline of Spirituality: Revisiting Questions of Definition and Method," *Spiritus* 1(2001): 65-78.

Rieff, Phillip. *Charisma: The Gift of Grace and How It Has Been Taken Away from Us*. New York: Pantheon Books, 2007.

Schneiders, Sandra M. "Religion vs. Spirituality: A Contemporary Conundrum," *Spiritus* 3 (2003), 163-85.

Smith, Wilfred Cantwell. *The Meaning and End of Religion*. New York: Macmillan, 1962.

Wach, Joachim. *The Comparative Study of Religion*. Edited with an introduction by Joseph M. Kitagawa. New York: Columbia University Press, 1958.

S. Daniel Breslauer

Dr. S. Daniel Breslauer is Emeritus Professor of Religious Studies at the University of Kansas in Lawrence. Dr. Breslauer received his Ph.D. in Near Eastern and Judaic Studies from Brandeis University in Waltham, Massachusetts.